AID AND INFLUENCE

ALSO BY JUST FAALAND

Essays on the Theory of Trade Discrimination, Chr. Michelsen Institute, Bergen, 1964

Bangladesh: the Test Case of Development, C. Hurst and Company, London, 1976 (with J. R. Parkinson)

Growth, Employment and Equity: a Comprehensive Strategy for the Sudan, International Labour Office, 1976 (as Chief of Mission)

ALSO BY NURUL ISLAM

Studies in Foreign Capital and Economic Development, Charles Tuttle and Co., Vermont, 1960

Financial Resources and Development Potential of East Pakistan, Government of East Pakistan, Dacca, 1962

A Short-Term Model for Pakistan's Economy: an Econometric Analysis, Oxford University Press, London, 1964

Studies in Consumer Demand, Vols I and II, Oxford University Press, Dacca, 1965–6

Development Planning in Bangladesh: a Study in Political Economy, C. Hurst and Company, London, 1977

ALSO BY JACK PARKINSON

The Economics of Shipbuilding in the United Kingdom, Cambridge University Press, 1960

Business Economics (with James Bates), Basil Blackwell (2nd edition, 1969)

Agricultural Co-operation in Northern Ireland, Cmd 484, HMSO, Belfast, 1965

Northern Ireland Development Programme, 1970–75, HMSO 1970 (with Professor Sir Robert Matthew and Professor Thomas Wilson)

Bangladesh: the Test Cast of Development, London, 1976 (with Just Faaland; see above)

AID AND INFLUENCE

The Case of Bangladesh

Edited by

Just Faaland

The Chr. Michelsen Institute, Bergen, Norway

Contributors

Just Faaland
Nurul Islam
Jack Parkinson

First published 1981 by
THE MACMILLAN PRESS LTD
London and Basingstoke
Companies and representatives throughout the world

Printed in Hong Kong

ISBN 0 333 28985 4

Contents

List of Tables

List of Abbreviations

United Nations Organisations

UN	United Nations
IBRD/World Bank	International Bank for Reconstruction and Development
IDA	International Development Association
IMF	International Monetary Fund
UNFPA	United Nations Fund for Population Activities
UNROB	United Nations Special Relief Office in Bangladesh
UNROD	United Nations Relief Operations Dacca
NIEO	New International Economic Order

International Agencies

EEC	European Economic Community
OECD	Organisation for Economic Cooperation and Development
DAC	Development Assistance Committee
OPEC	Organisation of Petroleum Exporting Countries

National Assistance Agencies

CIDA	Canadian International Assistance Agency
DTH	Netherlands Ministry of Development Cooperation (International Technical Assistance Department)
SIDA	Swedish International Development Agency
USAID	United States Agency for International Development

BADC	Bangladesh Agricultural Development Corporation

General

PVC	Polyvinyl Chloride
SDR	Special Drawing Rights

Preface

The call for a New International Economic Order (NIEO), so much on the agenda of the United Nations, covers the whole range of interrelationships between industrialised and developing countries, but the focus is mainly on the structure and terms of international trade. Important as this is, many of the poorest developing countries will find a new order of international trade, even one radically different from the present, at the best irrelevant to their most urgent needs. For the poorest countries, and Bangladesh prominently among them, the amount of foreign assistance, and the terms on which it is given, will remain for many years the decisive external factor in their efforts to overcome the massive deprivation and poverty of their populations. Seen in this perspective, this book is meant to contribute to the discussion of the New International Economic Order. If bilateral and international policies and institutions are ill suited to ensure effective aid relationships, the whole concept of aid as a contribution to improvement in international economic relationships may turn out to be defective.

An examination of the relations between Bangladesh and the international aid community is particularly instructive because they had to be developed from scratch. As a newly sovereign state, where the most dominant socio-political reality was the experience of long periods of rule by Britain and then domination by Pakistan, followed by a violent transition to political independence, the nature and form of the country's external relations were matters of great moment. The issue of reliance on foreign aid was hotly debated and contested in Bangladesh because of its international as well as domestic ramifications. National governments and international institutions concerned with aid were also faced with a new situation and with a test of the relevance and effectiveness of their established procedures and styles of operation. The issues that emerged in the process of seeking mutual accommodation are of general interest.

I therefore decided to seek to put together a set of accounts of experience and insight gained from the actual operation of aid relationships in Bangladesh. I invited contributions to this volume from two specialists in the field, Professors Nurul Islam and Jack Parkinson, and added a few chapters of my own. We have each reviewed separate and distinct aspects and issues of the development of aid relationships as they affected the country. Each of us has taken particular parts of the picture as his own exclusive responsibility. Professor Nurul Islam has written chapters 2, 4, 5 and 6, while Professor Parkinson has prepared chapters 3, 7, 10 and 11; the other four chapters have been written by myself.

As editor I have had the responsibility for decisions on the structure and the integration of the work of the three authors into a coherent whole. Each of us has taken his own approach in the review and analysis of the issues and problems we deal with in our respective chapters. This has required some rearrangement of material, as well as accommodation in form and scope of argument within chapters. In carrying out my editorial duties I was very grateful to my two colleagues for their co-operation and understanding. While we have discussed our views, there has been no occasion or need to seek to reconcile our differences. Moreover I have not seen it as part of my editorial duty to highlight such differences, or to gloss over them by choice of word or turn of phrase.

Professors Islam and Parkinson, as well as I myself, have benefited greatly when writing our chapters from our associations with the Chr. Michelsen Institute. During the Spring semester of 1977, when Professor Nurul Islam worked on his contributions to this volume, he was a visiting fellow of the Institute; similarly Professor Parkinson has been a frequent visitor. We all gratefully acknowledge the assistance of the librarian of the Institute and that of an indefatigable secretarial staff.

Bergen, 7 March 1979 Just Faaland

Part One:

The Story and its Setting

1 The Story

JUST FAALAND

In a few years, certainly within the 1980s, Bangladesh will have a population of well over 100 million. It will remain one of the lowest income countries in the world, and, barring major upheavals or revolutionary changes in its social and political outlook, it will remain the test case of economic development by combined internal effort and external assistance. Foreign aid commited to Bangladesh in the 1970s is likely to exceed US$ 8 billion; in 1977–8 alone it reached $1200 million, most of it as grants or on concessional terms. While aid on this scale to a single country represents a significant share of the world's total foreign assistance, the sums are not large by other standards: the annual net resource flow to Bangladesh is roughly twice the loss made in a bad year by the British Steel Corporation, and of the same order as the annual investment outlays by individual major transnational corporations. While the income supplement represented by foreign aid at current levels may average up to 15 per cent for the population in Bangladesh, it could be financed by Norway alone at the cost of a mere 3 per cent to 4 per cent of its national income, i.e. little more than the increase within a single year in the standard of living of that small but rich country.

In a country as poor as Bangladesh, foreign assistance at current levels, if reasonably effectively used and distributed, can make a very considerable difference to life and to development. For a population living at the margin of subsistence and with recurrent exposure to the threat of starvation, foreign assistance generally, and food and other commodity aid in particular, can make all the difference. It is this that makes it so necessary to exercise with circumspection and delicacy the power it puts into the hands of donors. The temptation to use it with the intention of improving Bangladesh's lot is all the greater because Bangladesh lacks so many of the means to develop that are available in abundance in the developed world. In Bangladesh there appears to be a dearth of people capable of designing and operating workable development projects or even policies and programmes for efficient operation of the economy, and those that are, inevitably start with the handicap that they do not have the supporting services and the resources of large and established institutions on which to draw. The political complexion of government is often uncertain and tends to be affected by many pressures which to an observer from abroad may seem to frustrate the needs of economic change. The problems of development are so great and so urgent that aid-givers often see this both as an opportunity and as a challenge to themselves to promote development using the resources that they can provide. Such actions may sometimes be counterproductive even though prompted by the best of intentions. Not all attempts to intervene are well intentioned however, and a country so heavily dependent on aid as Bangladesh can be made to suffer or to conform if there is a divergence of view between those who give and those who receive. These consequences are, of course, less apparent when foreign assistance is on a modest scale. For Bangladesh as now constituted, socially and politically, I do not believe it to be either possible or desirable to seek to attempt to develop her economy without sustained external assistance for a great many years on something like its present scale. This makes it all the more important to try to establish and sustain aid relationships that are efficient in terms of agreed objectives of both Bangladesh herself and the international aid community, and to do so with a deeper understanding and an explicit recognition of the problems that aid relationships of the type described in this book can bring in their train.

Our account is not concerned with the general issues of policies and planning, problems and potentials of development of Bangladesh; we have examined these at length elsewhere.[1] We are concerned here solely with the aid relationship: how it has developed, the problems that have been encountered in conducting international intercourse on this basis, and the lessons that may be learnt from this experience. Influence in aid relationships takes many forms and is of a shifting nature.

Sovereign governments naturally prefer to be independent of external influences on their affairs, and Bangladesh was no exception. As Bangladesh was a new country and its government and administration was feeling its way, aid relationships had to be developed from scratch. Initially this presented few problems for the flow of aid, for reconstruction of the economy was fashioned by the United Nations (UN) and administered first by United Nations Relief Operations Dacca (UNROD) and later by its successor United Nations Special Relief Office in Bangladesh (UNROB).[2] The stay of the United Nations Organisation was prolonged at the request of the Bangladesh Government; it had been, on the whole, satisfied with the UN's work and wished to prolong its presence until it became clear that the organisation built up for securing assistance was no longer needed and that the distribution of aid and particularly of food supplies, could be effectively operated by Bangladesh's own institutions and by local personnel.

As the United Nations operation faded out of the picture, it became increasingly important to establish aid relationships with other agencies and countries in addition to UN agencies such as the International Bank for Reconstruction and Development (IBRD/World Bank) and the International Monetary Fund (IMF) that could be counted on to sustain the economy as the transition from war time conditions to those of peace progressed. It was necessary for both Bangladesh and those supporting her to decide how best they could work together. There was much to learn, many false starts and difficulties, and many uncertainties.

With the preparation of the First Five Year Plan for Bangladesh in 1972–3, the issue of the scale on which assistance would be needed in the future came to the fore. The Plan was drawn up to rely on a limited amount of aid, which was projected to decrease rapidly over a given period, in a conscious and determined effort to minimise the influence of outsiders on the economy. Time was to show that this intention could not become reality. The situation evolved economically, socially and politically in a way that left few options open: it was better to depend on aid than to starve; it was better to have the prospect of development at a rate sufficient to escape the poverty trap than to refuse to face up to the problem of establishing satisfactory relationships with donors. In these conditions, good working relations with bilateral and multilateral sources of aid increasingly came to be realised in Bangladesh as being of great importance. The process of accommodation was painful on both sides, yet progress was made. Some problems once settled did not need to be reconsidered year by year, but as in all relationships things changed as time went on; objectives and procedures needed to be adjusted, new problems emerged as did new solutions; adjustment was a continuous process.

An illustration of this is provided by the need to apportion the flow of aid between types of resources to meet the circumstances and needs of Bangladesh more effectively. It was necessary to seek to convince those providing aid that an increased and more regular flow of commodities was a vital element of assistance to Bangladesh. There was little point in spending money on projects if the means to run them could not be found and if output could not be increased to provide the resources to invest in the future. Eventually this was recognised by donors who have increasingly shown a readiness to finance imports needed for the general support of the economy. Bangladesh, in turn, had to adjust to the exasperations of those providing commodity aid, when administrative procedures held up the arrival of badly needed imports, not only because of inefficiencies and inexperience in Bangladesh, but also because of the time needed to accommodate to the variety of operational procedures and requirements of different donors.

The relationships that had to be established were not just those between aid-givers and the recipient. A number of special interests had to be accommodated. Sometimes these related to suppliers in the donor countries, anxious to create conditions conducive to the sale of their products or expertise by political as well as commercial intervention. The provision of aid is regarded as an opportunity for the industries in the countries providing it, as well as for those wishing to receive it, to extract benefits for themselves in the process. The total of aid made available by a country sometimes had to be spread between its suppliers in a fashion which reflected their respective market situations and power to exert influence on the authorities of their own countries, and yet, somehow, Bangladesh had to reconcile this with its priorities for assistance in the provision of particular raw materials and commodities for the special needs of its industries, railways or airline. The ministries in Bangladesh and the field agencies watched these allocations with care; they too had their interests. They were not averse to trying to influence the allocation of aid by joining forces with donors and suppliers' agents in an endeavour to push their claims by an exercise of influence, and thus to get the kind of equipment they felt to be best suited to their needs. It is instructive to review these matters in specific cases which illustrate such problems of aid allocation, as well as the ways in which attempts were made to seek solutions to conflicting requirements and interests.

It was soon found that donors did not hesitate to impose detailed conditions on the aid that they bestowed. They wished to be sure that their aid would be effective, and they were generally distrustful of the readiness and ability of Bangladesh to ensure this unless donors stipulated explicit conditions in an effort to enforce compliance with the legal framework of formal agreement. The most trying aspect was the imposition of conditions concerned with the management and administration of projects. At times, efforts to do so were regarded by Bangladesh as little less than attempts to interfere in the sovereignty of the country. Such tactics are always liable to be defeated; even with apparent acceptance of administrative stipulations, their implementation can be frustrated by delay or imperfect execution and the net result may be counterproductive in every way, including the loss of time of negotiating teams.

There was considerable reluctance on the part of donors to supply commodities in the form of unconditional aid. While the need to work out the viability of projects before loans are granted for them is readily seen, it might be felt that supply or finance of commodity imports would be subject to much less scrutiny. This is not the case; the procedures for dealing with such programmes are complex and the justification for them has to be detailed and related to the type of commodity that it is intended to import; in fact more information and more searching enquiries may be made in the case of commodity credits than in the case of projects.

Of prime importance in the provision of commodity aid was supplies of food. This gave rise to considerable problems, starting with that of trying to estimate the extent of requirements, given all the uncertainties of harvest prospects. It continued with the need to try to find sources of supply and determine how much would be provided under aid programmes and how much would be purchased by Bangladesh out of her own resources. Supply lines were long and liable to be interrupted; it was difficult to find additional supplies at short notice if the harvest failed disastrously, and the consequences of failing to do so were drastic. Donor countries were far from satisfied with the distribution system for food. They were especially critical of the system of rationing that was in force which favoured the relatively affluent in urban areas and the advantaged factions of government and the armed forces, rather than the landless and workless. The points of view of donors and the Bangladesh authorities were as far apart with regard to the rationing system, as they were in relation to the ineffective (as they saw it) system of procurement of food from farmers as a source of supply for the towns. It was Bangladesh's dependence on food aid that finally, in 1974, most clearly demonstrated the ultimate sanction which major donors hold on the recipient country, both in terms of limiting its freedom of action in internal policy and in its foreign relations.

Problems experienced in bilateral relations were dwarfed by those with multilateral dimensions. The formation of a regular donor consortium was not welcomed by Bangladesh; it was the donors who felt the need for co-ordination of their activities and who from the first pressed for the establishment of a consortium. Bangladesh was much more doubtful of the wisdom of such an arrangement and the benefits that it might have for her; there was, however, a readiness to consider it as a possible way of organising aid programmes. The wishes of donors in this respect might have been met at an early stage if they had been prepared to accept a modified form of consortium of the type that was experimented with in a meeting organised in Dacca in March 1973. While this experiment was successful in demonstrating that local meetings could be an alternative to the standard International Bank for Reconstruction and Development (IBRD/World Bank) consortia meetings usually held in Paris, the Dacca meeting was a failure in another respect: the proceedings were dominated by the determination of donor delegations to use the occasion to bring pressure to bear on Bangladesh to accept liability for debts contracted by Pakistan prior to 1971. This threatened to disrupt relations completely.

It was the object of donors to induce Bangladesh to accept the obligation of servicing some of the international debt contracted by Pakistan before Bangladesh attained its independence. Donor countries organised by the World Bank acted in concert with the object of persuading Bangladesh to accept what she considered an unwarranted obligation. Their representatives clearly felt that with her great need for aid Bangladesh would be certain to give in to their demands. This expectation was mistaken and they did not succeed. Their case was untenable and Bangladesh declined to accede to their views. The consequences of this experience of donor pressure on the aid recipient, and of the way it was organised and exercised, disrupted relations with major donors generally and the World Bank in particular. In the course of 1973–4, it was, nevertheless, possible to reach a compromise agreement which gave the donors something of what they wanted, and at the same time, did not seem to Bangladesh to violate the principles she felt it most important should be observed. The resolution of this tendentious issue was helped by the eventual recognition of Bangladesh by Pakistan, for it was intimately bound up with political issues arising out of the war. It is an important case study, which shows donors all too willing to use the leverage they possess in relation to a poor country. In this case, the willingness of Bangladesh to settle the issue was not primarily a reflection of economic compulsion, which often forced her to accept the exigencies of donors, so much as an expedient response that became appropriate as the political situation in the sub-continent evolved.

There can be little negotiating power when economic need is paramount. No country can have been worse hit than Bangladesh by the rise in the price of oil and foodstuffs which affected her with increasing severity in 1974 when the general weakness of her economy was all too apparent. Bangladesh simply could not afford to buy the imports to keep her economy running and was without the means to fend off starvation. The economy was at crisis point.

This presaged a series of changes in Bangladesh's relations with donors. Perhaps the least of these was the necessity of accepting the formation of an old style consortium where donors would have a forum in which they could regularly subject the economy of Bangladesh and the policies of its Government to collective scrutiny. Donors' influence on Bangladesh's affairs was formally recognised and accepted; it had been intense before and might be more controllable in organised meetings at which Bangladesh was formally represented. It did, however, serve to remind Bangladesh of the importance of the World Bank as a co-ordinator in the minds of Western donors.

The dominance of the Bank is seen in almost all developments unfolded in this story. It is regarded by donors as the authority on policies to be followed by developing countries; in fact, donors appear much more inclined to pay attention to the views of the Bank than they are to those of the countries concerned. An ill-considered or uninformed World Bank report can therefore do considerable harm to the aid recipient, particularly when, as in the case of a major report on Bangladesh, insult is added to injury. Nobody enjoys reading disparaging remarks about their country, particularly when advanced without understanding in official reports, and without regard to the usages of diplomacy – and Bengalis are as sensitive to criticism as anyone else.

The Bank is a powerful influence on the design of the strategy for development adopted by developing countries, and this extends to project selection and to the preparation and implementation of projects, as well as to the design and organisation of major programme areas. Various chapters illustrate the force and form of the Bank's exercise of its influence on decision making within Bangladesh and describe how it affected the views and actions of donors in respect of a major petro-chemical project, and the country's population planning programme.

The role of the International Monetary Fund (IMF) appears less pervasive in developing countries than that of the Bank. Its major preoccupations are with finance, both internal and external, and particularly with the appropriateness of the exchange rate. In these areas, the Fund's reports are considered authoritative and have considerable influence on the climate of opinion in the international aid community. The Fund's particular concern in Bangladesh was with exchange rate policy. From 1972 onwards the Fund consistently held the view that the Taka was overvalued and that devaluation should be undertaken immediately. Bangladesh was reluctant to do so.

Even though there was a meeting of minds on the basic merits of devaluation, Bangladesh resisted and refrained from devaluation for three years. The debate with the Fund (often quite technical) related not only to devaluation itself, but also revealed important differences of view with respect to the nature of the foreign exchange system which Bangladesh preferred to operate. However, following the difficulties experienced in 1974–5, Bangladesh had no real option but to seek an arrangement with the Fund in return for being allowed to borrow further tranches of its quota. Devaluation finally took place in May 1975 when the worst of the financial crisis was over.

The account of aid donor–recipient relationships in Bangladesh, if properly understood and interpreted, may yield lessons of value for the conduct of such relationships in the future; in the final chapter some of these matters are dealt with in a wider setting. Here it suffices to stress and describe the profound impact which relationships with the international aid community had on Bangladesh from its inception.

The story related in the following chapters shows that a country as heavily dependent as Bangladesh on foreign assistance, cannot escape continuous participation by donors in the formulation of its policies. It may prepare its five year and annual plans, its minister of finance may draw up his budget, the ministries may make their programmes, but all do so with the consciousness that dominant aid agencies are looking over their shoulders.

The World Bank will seek to participate both by discussion and by studies of its own in the making of national plans; and later when plans are completed it will continue to make critical comment on every aspect of them. The Bank reviews national plans in such a manner and form, and so thoroughly and comprehensively, that individual donor governments sometimes fail to distinguish the Bank's critical studies of such plans from the plans themselves. The Bank's scrutiny includes a comprehensive review of all major policy measures, critically examining fiscal proposals for their adequacies and deficiencies, for their effects on equity, and in relation to the capability of the revenue departments of putting them into effect. It looks equally critically at the functioning of the banking sector and the demands that the government may place on it for finance.

The Fund in turn pronounces on the government's financial policies and delivers its verdict on exchange rate policy, often, it may be felt, with the preconceived view that the currency will be overvalued and, invariably, that the time for devaluation is now. If this is its view, it will not hesitate to insist on change and to enforce it if the country is sufficiently pressed by circumstance to be driven to ask it for finance. None outside the country is likely to dissent from the Fund's view or the need to carry it into effect.

These forces to refashion the policies of the country are not applied once and for all; they are continuous; each budget, each new plan, each consortium meeting presents a new opportunity for dialogue and cumulative influence by the international aid community designed to achieve its ends. The dialogue is not confined to economic issues; it ranges widely over the nature and structure of the economy, generally as viewed through Western eyes.

The exercise of influence extends beyond the consideration of major policy issues. Every aspect of the economy is subject to the same detailed scrutiny and prescription. In Bangladesh, the British designed and advised on two-thirds of the industrial sector, providing jute machinery and the technical means to operate it; and Government credits sought to ensure that management practices bore some resemblances to those of Dundee and to the recommendations of industrial consultants called in to advise on management structures from the level of the ministry itself to the Khulna shop floor. The transport system was both assisted by and subjected to the advice of the Economist Intelligence Unit, while the country's system of transport operations, whether sea, road, rail or air, were planned to approximate to those practised in the countries supplying equipment. The French designed the airport, the Russians and others the power supply, UNROD and the Canadians gave guidance and even took over direct responsibility for the movement of goods and people. The World Bank arranged for the building of a fertiliser factory, but effectively barred the establishment of a petro-chemical complex; foreigners prospected for oil.

The need for food exerted a stranglehold on the whole economy. The new technologies were developed and imported from overseas, including those for the production of rice. The production inputs needed were provided under aid according to the availability of surpluses and the generosity or interest of donors. The development strategy for agriculture devised by Bangladesh was influenced by a dialogue with the World Bank specialist teams who surveyed the possibilities with a thoroughness and competence never before displayed; the hardcore programme for agriculture, pointing the way for future action, emerged almost as a by-product of this activity.

The attention of foreigners is not confined to material welfare. Health, education and family planning pass under their scrutiny as they analyse, criticise, advise, innovate and experiment in areas where they cannot have any certain knowledge of the consequences of the policies they advocate. One undesirable result of all this foreign participation is that it can have the effect of blunting initiative as well as creating dependence on the part of the country concerned.

The evidence from experience of the influence and dominance by the aid-givers over recipients is that it can have results that are unintended and undesirable in terms of the purpose of aid given for development. Constant subjection to outside advice and oversight holds back the emergence of such self-reliance and confidence in the management of affairs which can make poverty more bearable and pave the way for self-sustained development.

Notes

1. See for example, Nurul Islam, *Development Planning in Bangladesh, A Study in Political Economy*, C. Hurst & Co., London, 1977 and Just Faaland and J. R. Parkinson, *Bangladesh: the Test Case of Development*, C. Hurst & Co., London, 1976.
2. A semi-official account of these UN operations is given in T. W. Oliver, *United Nations in Bangladesh*, Princeton University Press, 1978. An interesting review prepared in 1974–5 by W. F. Hughes has been available to this writer, but the manuscript does not seem to have been published.

2 The Debate

NURUL ISLAM

Bangladesh was born in December 1971 out of a war of liberation – a war in which many died and many more suffered extreme privation. Thirty million people were forced to leave their homes and move elsewhere in the country, or to India where ten million found refuge. Damage was extensive. The physical damage resulting from the war of liberation was estimated to have been well over $1500 million,[1] excluding loss of current output.

Within a month of the war's ending the United Nations set up a relief organisation in Dacca to alleviate suffering by providing assistance, including food and shelter, to civilian victims. Shortly after independence, the United Nations sent a mission to Bangladesh to assess the need for foreign assistance with rehabilitation and reconstruction. The first requirement was for emergency supplies of food and the means to overcome damage to transport systems and communications so that supplies could be distributed. It was estimated that in the first year nearly $300 million would be needed for emergency imports of food, mainly grain and edible oil. The immediate reaction of the United Nations Secretary General was to make a world-wide appeal for assistance in the provision and distribution of food. It was furnished in quantity, particularly by India. The United Nations mission considered that for the period from independence to mid-1973 a minimum of $650 million of other assistance would be required for reconstruction. To this need also there was a generous response.

The immediate help proffered by the United Nations for relief and reconstruction of the economy was accepted gratefully by all parties in Bangladesh, as was that received from India. Without it, there would have been prolonged suffering, and it was given freely on humanitarian grounds and without political implications. The prospect of dependence on outside assistance for economic and social development, once reconstruction had been accomplished, was another matter; on this there were differing views. The official policy announced by the Prime Minister early in 1972 was that Bangladesh would accept assistance from all friendly countries so long as no 'strings' were attached. Such statements are seldom free from ambiguity. It was unlikely that foreign aid in the 1970s would be made openly dependent on the acceptance of political conditions; the underlying issues which influenced the thinking of politicians in Bangladesh were more subtle though no less clearly understood for that. There were both ideological and pragmatic pulls and pressures in diverse directions within the upper echelons of the political leadership of the country; this was particularly evident after independence in 1972. The considerations discussed below were given various degrees of importance by those involved in the debate.

There was first the issue of relations with the United States, which clearly regarded aid as an important element in its world strategy and was known to have cut it off when countries pursued policies that did not meet with its approval. The crucial issue in assessing future relationships was not really the past record of the United States in aid-giving, or that it might not approve of the sort of policies that Bangladesh would wish to pursue, so much as the fact that during the war of independence the United States had a pronounced leaning in favour of Pakistan and had no sympathy for the creation of an independent state of Bangladesh.[2]

This experience of attitudes and actions of the United States, as perceived by Bangladesh at independence, also coloured views in Bangladesh on the role of the World Bank. There was in the minds of policy makers in Bangladesh, however justifiably or otherwise, a close association between the Bank and its most important and dominant member, the United States, and it was known that there was an understanding between the members of the Bank that its President should be (as has always been the case) an American.

Relations with the Soviet Union and India were other major issues. India looked to Russia for support, not least against China. In 1972, the support of both these countries for Bangladesh during the war of independence was very much in mind. China, in 1971, showed no sign of friendship and stood between Bangladesh and recognition in the United Nations. The indications of a readiness to furnish political support and economic assistance had come from the Soviet Union. After Sheik Mujibur Rahman[3] was released from prison in Pakistan he was immediately invited to visit Russia, where there were a series of discussions on aid and other bilateral relationships and specifically on the provisions of trawlers, the clearance of mines and the finance for projects which had been started but not finished.

Early in 1972, when only a few countries recognised the independent state of Bangladesh and fewer still had diplomatic representation, assistance was provided mainly under the auspices of the United Nations. The first bilateral aid agreements signed at that time were with the Soviet Union and India. The United States, for reasons already explained, was not in favour. While the considerable assistance it had given immediately after independence with food and in other ways had come without political strings, the future would not hold out such a prospect. At this point it looked as if Bangladesh might seek to stay largely outside the sphere of Western economic influence. Also, there was a feeling that it would be possible, if not to go it alone, at least to survive and eventually progress mainly by national efforts, supplemented by the relatively small amounts of aid that could be obtained from the Soviet bloc and from non-aligned friendly countries. The USSR apparently would have been prepared to have given Bangladesh continued support and had shown great cordiality to its Prime Minister. However, Bangladesh was not entirely willing to align itself with any foreign power in such a way as to impair Bangladesh's freedom to determine its own future: it wished to keep its options open. As the euphoria of victory in the fight for independence faded, doubts arose as to whether Bangladesh could survive without large-scale assistance, which could come only from the West. The decisive issue became clear: should Bangladesh's relationships with foreign countries be shaped in such a way as to secure and rely on significant assistance for survival and development, or were other considerations paramount?

Most developing countries are faced with issues such as this as they struggle to accelerate their growth. Not all have decided to accept reliance on foreign assistance; but those that have, find that dependence on aid, once accepted, is not easy to cast off.

Bangladesh, a new country, was doubtful about the wisdom of accepting the offerings of others and wished to consider the options before her with care before deciding what to do. When Bangladesh emerged as an independent nation people were thought to be prepared to bear such sacrifices as might be required of them to sustain the sovereignty of their country and government; this made it less necessary to choose the apparently easiest road to development, based on the acceptance of large amounts of aid from the West, rather than that of self-reliance supported by only a modicum of foreign assistance. Nevertheless, there were strong political compulsions working in the other direction. The administrative structure and modern organised sector of industry had been built up during Pakistani rule on the basis of a level of imports and public expenditure beyond the capabilities of the domestic economy and its revenue raising resources. The needs of the urban/industrial classes anywhere are liable to shape the pattern of political evolution, so also in Bangladesh.

If aid were to be accepted, the alternatives were either to depend heavily on the West, in the expectation that this would bring with it large amounts of assistance, or to avoid such dependence, in the knowledge that economic support could be expected only in modest proportion from the Eastern bloc, probably also only for a limited period, and that a correspondingly greater effort would be needed domestically. The nature of the support offered would also be different. For Bangladesh the need, even after emergency requirements had been met, would be for flexible support in the form of commodity aid. For many things the Western donors were the only source of supply. Aid in the form of food, fertilisers, pesticides and industrial raw materials was available in significant quantities only from the United States of America and other Western countries. India, which had provided massive food aid in 1972, could not afford to continue to do so. The Eastern bloc of countries could at best be relied upon to provide commodities under trade agreements; otherwise they were known to prefer to concentrate on project assistance. The apparent readiness of the USSR to establish friendly relations with Bangladesh widened the options available to Bangladesh although it did not in any way settle the issue of what strategy to adopt with respect to Bangladesh's dependence on foreign assistance.

In 1972 it was widely believed in Bangladesh that once reconstruction was accomplished, most, if not all resources for development would be available from within the domestic economy. During much of the time when Bangladesh had formed part of Pakistan it had in fact generated significant savings and resources for development which had been diverted to West Pakistan and used there. There would be no such drain after independence and both domestic savings and foreign exchange earnings would be under the control of Bangladesh itself for the development of the economy. It was assumed that this would obviate the need to rely on large amounts of foreign assistance to support the development effort. This view was mistaken. By the mid-sixties the transfer of resources from Bangladesh to West Pakistan had been on the wane; twenty years of inadequate investment had taken its toll. *Per capita* income had not shown the increase registered in West Pakistan; population had been increasing more rapidly than agricultural production; the capacity to produce a surplus for investment on the scale needed was no longer there. The need for external assistance was increasingly evident.

By the time the First Five Year Plan was formulated in 1972–3, it was realised by the Government that significant dependence on foreign aid, at least for some years, was indispensable for even a moderate increase in *per capita* income to be achieved. The Annual Plan for 1972/73 and the First Five Year Plan accepted the need for aid, but conveyed the message that large-scale reliance on foreign aid initially must be used to create the capacity for subsequent reduction of dependence on outside assistance and for greater self-reliance. Behind this attitude lay the fear that the greater the dependence on foreign aid, the greater the likelihood of interference by donor countries in the political and economic life of Bangladesh, as had happened with other countries. It was regarded as axiomatic that there was a conflict between reliance on foreign aid and the maintenance of freedom and flexibility in determining political and economic policies.

Another facet of the desire to minimise exposure to influence derived from dependence on aid was that sources of foreign economic assistance needed to be as diversified as possible. Heavy dependence on aid from a single big power was more likely to encourage political and economic pressures than aid provided by a number of smaller countries which were not politically or economically important in international affairs. In this respect small was beautiful, but it introduced the dilemma that the objective could be attained only if the need for aid could be confined to what could be provided in this way; if it could not, there was no escape from dependence on big and powerful countries. This, of course, is not an issue in any sense peculiar to Bangladesh. What is of relevance here are the particular considerations and turn of events that affected the options available and – it seemed inevitably – led Bangladesh to accept reliance on massive international aid.

In political circles and elsewhere it was being asked whether the commitment of Bangladesh to socialism was consistent with dependence on aid from the non-socialist countries. In fact, however, there was little evidence of any dogmatic doctrinaire socialist ideology emerging as a dominant element. It was not easy to see how a political party composed of *bourgeoisie*, spearheading a nationalist independence movement, could be either ideologically committed to socialism as a way of organising economic and political life, or capable of accomplishing a socialist transformation of Bangladesh.

Those who were against large-scale dependence on aid from the major Western countries argued that such dependence was inconsistent with the building up of a socialist Bangladesh and that economic assistance, even without overt political or ideological strings, carried political implications with it. The argument that doctrinaire socialist countries in Eastern Europe were themselves involved in accepting loans and technical assistance from the non-socialist world carried little weight, for the amount was very limited and confined to certain spheres of activity. Such interchanges did not take the form of concessional assistance but were strictly commercial deals; they did not entail the close involvement of donors in discussions on the economic system and economic policy matters. Mature socialist countries could be expected to resist outside influence; but in their early days, when the foundations of socialism were in the process of being built, intercourse with the non-socialist world was severely restricted. The influence of an alien ideology or economic system was more likely to be important in the formative years when there was no widely accepted and well-grounded view about the desired pattern of society.

In counter argument, it would not be hard to reject the views of those opposing involvement with non-socialist countries, if it could be assumed that Bangladesh was determined to follow its chosen ideology and if donor countries were willing to provide assistance within this framework in a way that could be accepted with confidence. It was the internal strength of convictions that was crucial. If this existed, the flow of economic and technical assistance was neither socialist nor non-socialist. It was the use which was made of such aid that made a country socialist or non-socialist.

Such arguments, however, did nothing to dispel anxiety about the effects of Western aid. In one respect, at least, they were weak; it related to the effect of foreign training on Bangladesh nationals. If it was intended to indoctrinate the younger generation with socialist ideas, training in non-socialist countries was not likely to promote this objective.[4] A willingness on the part of Bangladesh to send students to non-socialist as well as socialist countries, irrespective of whether they would study natural science, social sciences or arts, could be interpreted only as a readiness to encourage and perpetuate debate on the choice between conflicting economic and political systems in Bangladesh. Many took the view that sending students to study in the West would amount to no less than a positive decision to opt for a mixed economy and mixed ideology.

For the Planning Commission such debates needed to be translated into practical terms. What level and what composition of aid would be politically tolerable? Was it desirable to set a limit to the amount or proportion of aid that Bangladesh should accept from countries with a particular economic and political ideology so that no single socio-political system would have predominance in the provision of aid? The difficulty with this approach was that it would have restricted the availability of external assistance. As the foreign exchange shortage worsened in 1973, and the continued food shortage and world wide inflation made the import bill for necessities soar, the need for large-scale assistance became all too apparent, with the corollary that Bangladesh would become heavily dependent on the West. It was not that Bangladesh explicitly opted to maximise the flow of foreign economic assistance rather than choose a neatly balanced geographical distribution of a smaller amount of foreign assistance. Events got out of hand and left no freedom of action; the alternatives of self-reliance and only modest levels of assistance from socialist countries and small friendly countries had effectively disappeared.

Early in 1972, when aid relationships were in the course of being established on a continuing basis, it had been proposed by Western donors that an aid consortium for Bangladesh should be organised. The issue was a thorny one. Bangladesh, as we have seen, was anxious not to be identified so early in her history with what she considered to be a club of donors dominated by Western countries. There were, however, a number of reasons that could be advanced for the establishment of a consortium. The pre-independence consortium for Pakistan had worked quite well. Many of the countries represented on it had financed development projects in Bangladesh that were still to be completed; many of them had co-operated through the United Nations in the relief and rehabilitation operations undertaken in the immediate post-independence period. Assistance to Bangladesh was, to some extent, a continuing activity and it might seem natural to re-establish the familiar modes of operation.

Proponents of the consortium suggested that a common review of aid operations would prevent duplication of efforts and encourage countries to concentrate on those activities for which they were best suited. The World Bank could provide regular reviews of the Bangladesh economy which would be more thorough than individual donor countries could hope to accomplish with limited resources. These reviews would establish the magnitude of the aid needed and provide a basis for discussing strategies and policies. In the process, the views of individual donors on development objectives and priorities would be harmonised and a common approach to solving Bangladesh's problems agreed. It was suggested that this might also help to get over the problem that individual projects, however well conceived and executed, could not expect to yield maximum returns unless the economy as a whole operated effectively. For example, donors providing food in substantial amounts might wish to know how their operations were likely to affect agricultural performance and to be involved in discussions on investment in agriculture and consulted on policies for increasing production in that sector.[5]

From another point of view, the exchanges between donors at the meetings of a consortium (and in the preparatory and subsequent work associated with it) might be expected to be of value in harmonising the attitudes of the donors themselves. On a wider scale, it would be likely to lead to a more equitable sharing of the aid burden amongst donors, and a joint collaborative approach could be expected to make it easier for aid programmes to be justified before legislatures of donor countries. A common effort often carries the conviction that what is proposed must be right because it represents the view of others who are thought to be in a better position to judge, in this case the most active donor and chairman of the consortium, the World Bank.

It was maintained that such considerations would work strongly to Bangladesh's advantage. Her need for assistance would be put forcibly to a receptive forum. Convinced believers in the desirability of helping Bangladesh would be able to bring their influence to bear and whip the laggards along with the ride. Hard donors would be shamed into giving soft assistance by the insistence of those prepared to offer easy terms. Above all, there would be a greater certainty of aid in sufficient quantities and a greater certainty of its continuity, which would improve the efficiency of economic planning.

It may seem strange in the face of all these arguments that Bangladesh was not enthusiastic about the formation of a consortium; yet, the very arguments that seemed to point in favour of a consortium acted in some respects as a discouragement. The fact that a consortium would be likely to arrive at a common view about the strategies, policies and priorities for development in Bangladesh, opened up the possibility that more pressure would be exerted on her than if discussions were to be undertaken mainly on a bilateral basis. Flexibility and initiative would be lost if it were necessary to enunciate, defend and justify policies and priorities to a consortium. It would no longer be possible for Bangladesh to take advantage of the difference and divergencies in emphasis and approach which undoubtedly existed amongst donors, particularly in relation to institutional and constitutional matters. Once an economic forum was established, the more aggressive and active donors would dominate and, unless underlying differences were very strong, individual donors would seldom stand out against the general view. The desire to avoid uniformity of approach amongst donors could be regarded as a 'maximin strategy', an effort to avoid the worst befalling. There was the possibility that the influence of dominant donors might in the end be favourable to Bangladesh: reluctant donors might be made to give more under the influence of the more generous; but then again the hard-liners might get the upper hand. In the minds of the political leadership in Bangladesh the need to preserve bargaining and negotiating strength was uppermost.

The political implications of the establishment of a consortium of aid givers so soon after independence had to be considered by Bangladesh. The socialist countries, particularly the USSR, had supported Bangladesh strongly at independence, in international forums as well as bilaterally. The socialist countries had granted her diplomatic recognition speedily but many other countries had been slow to do so. Although by the beginning of 1973 most other countries had also taken this step, relationships had not been consolidated with any of them. There had been no opportunity to have an exchange of views on vital political matters and there was no certain means of knowing whether Bangladesh's declared adherence to an independent neutral foreign policy had been fully accepted. It was a period of hesitancy in foreign policy made more difficult by a feeling of insecurity in international relations.

The fact that the socialist countries would not be included in a consortium was therefore of political significance. Socialist countries, even those like Yugoslavia and Rumania who were members of the Bank, were reluctant to join consortia and coordinate their own efforts in this way.[6]

Notes

1. Source: UNROD, Dacca, and Government of Bangladesh, Planning Commission. See also *The Economic Development of Bangladesh within a Socialist Framework, Proceedings of a Conference held by the International Economic Association at Dacca.* Ed. by E. A. G. Robinson and Keith Griffin, London, Macmillan, 1974.
2. It will be recalled that towards the end of the civil war the United States Seventh Fleet sailed into the Bay of Bengal when the Pakistani army was still grimly hanging on; to some this seemed to symbolise the United States' attitude to Bangladesh.
3. Sheik Mujibur Rahman, the undisputed political leader of East Pakistan who had been imprisoned by Pakistani forces in late March 1971 assumed the office of Prime Minister on his return to Dacca in early January 1972.
4. Most individual students seem to be susceptible to accepting the norms to which they are exposed even though some like Marx, find it convenient to develop revolutionary ideas in the British Museum.
5. 'There are numerous cases in the history of aid in which a recipient had received conflicting advice from different aid-givers. If the recipient's

performance is to be made a criterion for the allocation of aid, and if that recipient depends on aid from more than one source, he might well be required to implement self contradictory policies in order to secure continuing aid. . . . ' 'The first need is for exposition . . . The reason why exposition is essential is that the aid-givers have to adopt a single external view of the recipient's needs to which they may individually address themselves. If the view that is adopted turns out to be wrong, or if a sharp difference of view emerges between the aid-givers and the recipient, further discussions can easily be initiated. But if the aid-givers adopt a welter of disparate views, even if one of them happens to be right, it is difficult to see how a meaningful aid relationship can develop.' John White, *Pledged to Development*. London, Overseas Development Institute, 1966, pp. 187 and 188.

6. They were in fact invited to the first Aid Group meeting in Paris and attended it but subsequently withdrew.

3 The Needs

JACK PARKINSON

The characteristics of the Bangladesh economy are described at length elsewhere[1] and only some of them are germane to an understanding of the issue discussed in this book. The overriding consideration is that of the poverty of the 85 million people who inhabit the country. There is a near Malthusian pressure on existence as population growth matches, and sometimes exceeds, the growth of output; there is little in the way of additional land that can be brought into cultivation in one of the most densely populated areas in the world. Nor can industrial production offer much immediate alternative to agriculture in the way of employment, or improving living standards. There are few natural resources that can be utilised as the basis of industrialisation (the best of these, jute, has only limited growth potential). There are few raw materials that can readily be extracted and easily sold on world markets as a means to secure foreign exchange. While export earning capacity is capable of expansion, the process is slow and earnings are sufficient to pay for less than a half of minimum import needs.

At the time to which the accounts in this book relate, starvation could be avoided only if adequate imports of food were forthcoming. Employment in many areas was dependent on imports of raw materials and manufactured goods. So also was the comfort of the influential ruling class, which was much more affected than the masses by the supply of foreign goods. Both directly and indirectly the speed at which economic development could be pursued depended on the flow of aid backed with elements of foreign expertise. Aid was thus vital to every aspect of the country's economy. In many respects, however, ready made foreign solutions could not be found for the country's difficulties. Development had to be concerned, above all, with the people living in their scattered villages, tilling the soil and in need as much of social transformation as of all that modern science and technology could do to improve yields and cultivation methods. This problem is not something that readily yields to technical and administrative measures or even to the provision of financial and material resources, for it involves every aspect of organisation of society and production.

The First Five Year Plan attempted to estimate import requirements and export receipts for the period 1973–8. In total it appeared that at 1972–3 prices about $2.4 million of foreign assistance would be needed before any provision was made for the service of debt. Requirements of aid year by year could not be fully worked out because of uncertainty about how agricultural production would be affected by the weather, but it was clearly intended to reduce dependence on aid progressively and rapidly. This was in keeping with the desire to avoid having to rely on foreign support, although it may also have been intended to convince donors that aid would increase production sufficiently to hold out the promise that Bangladesh would be able to provide for her own needs within a relatively short period. Contemporary criticism of the estimates of the balance of payments suggested that they were rather optimistic. The need for imports, including imports of food, was considered to be understated while estimates of exports, which assumed India's jute manufacturing industry would purchase from Bangladesh, were considered to be unattainable.

There could have been no more unfortunate time to have to finalise a plan that inevitably must be made on the basis of a whole set of estimates and assumptions: a month after the plan was made public, oil prices escalated as did those of foodgrains and other imports. In the process the assumptions on which the balance of payments estimates had been drawn up were totally swept away.

If the economic crisis that assailed Bangladesh in 1973–4 could have been foreseen, there might have been less doubt within Government about the inevitability of dependency on aid. If the preparation of the plan had been less rushed and discussed at length within Government, its content might also have been modified in various ways.

The escalation of import prices could scarcely have been predicted but a more prescient assessment of social and political realities in Bangladesh would no doubt have produced a plan based on higher estimated foreign assistance. The economic difficulties of 1972 were only partly due to the aftermath of war. Underlying them lay the growing pressure of population on agricultural output, already evident in the increasing need for imports of food in the 1960s. The shortage of food and the need to buy it abroad was the root of Bangladesh's troubles. Bad harvests exposed Bangladesh's vulnerability to events with cumulative effect. One consequence was that land was diverted from the production of jute to rice so that exports of jute and jute manufactures languished; another, the drying up of supplies of even essential imports. These diffculties were compounded by others. The establishment of a functioning government with a rebuilt administrative structure was a considerable accomplishment made possible only by the adaptation of existing institutions; but inevitably administrative procedures and structures were deficient in many respects and this led to slowness in recognising what was happening in the economy and restricted the degree to which things could be put right once deficiencies had been revealed.

In retrospect it is clear that too sanguine a view was taken of the rate at which the economy would recover to previous levels of activity, and the restoration of a situation approximating to that of pre-war turned out to be measured more in terms of years than in the months that had been hoped. It was greatly extended by the adverse turn of international events in 1973, which so much dominated Bangladesh's external economic position and denuded her of foreign resources. This, more than anything else, forced the issue of external dependence on foreign assistance. The situation in which Bangladesh found herself in 1974, left no doubt that the country simply did not dispose of the resources to make a gradual transition to viability practicable in the absence of a large amount of foreign assistance. Short of a total and successful social revolution, the alternative was starvation, which nobody was prepared to countenance. As the situation deteriorated, the political and economic options closed up.

The slow recovery of the economy and its accompanying balance of payments crisis is all too evident from the statistics of the time. It took food production four years to recover to the level attained before the war and in the meantime population had increased by more than ten per cent. Production of jute in 1974–5 was only one-half of that in 1969–70 and has remained well below the pre-war level. The low returns from it in terms of importing capacity, continues to impede the development of the economy. Industrial activity, affected by the shortage of imports, damage, destruction and industrial unrest had on average regained pre-war levels by 1973–4 although output was rather differently constituted from formerly. Nevertheless mere recovery was quite insufficient to add impetus to development or to provide the basis for the kind of structural change that was needed to ease the balance of payments problem; industry, large- and small-scale, accounts for only 10 per cent of output in Bangladesh and its contribution to growth is correspondingly confined.

The deterioration in the international situation set off by the unprecedented movement in the terms of trade transcended domestic deficiencies. In the worst year, 1975–6, the index of the terms of trade showed that the purchasing power of exports had fallen to a little more than half of that in 1969–70. Few countries can have experienced such a fall in the international purchasing power of their exports over so short a period; moreover, in previous movements on this scale (at the time of the Korean war) the situation was rapidly restored to a more normal relationship. The improvement that has since taken place in Bangladesh's situation has been minimal; in 1976–7 only about 20 per cent of the original loss on the terms of trade had been regained and even in 1977–8, when the price of jute showed some recovery, the terms of trade were 25 per cent worse than in 1972–3. Bangladesh, which in 1969–70 had been able to pay for about 90 per cent of its visible imports from its own export receipts, could pay for little more than one quarter of her import requirements in 1974–5.

Such figures leave no doubt about the dependency of Bangladesh on external assistance. Throughout its existence Bangladesh has been heavily, sometimes almost totally, dependent on aid for the supply of imports of almost every category. During the period covered by the First Five Year Plan (1973–8) over 70 per cent of food and capital goods, and about 60 per cent of imports of intermediate goods, have in fact been paid for by foreign assistance.[2] Dependence extended also to Government finance. Foreign assistance, whether used directly or as a source of budgetary resources in the form of counterpart funds, has typically financed over 75 per cent of public development expenditure.[3] Effectively the rest of public development expenditure was financed by creating money. Since the alternative to this was to increase taxation in order to swell Government revenue, there were internal political considerations against trying to reduce dependence on aid once it had been established.

In practice the supplies of aid received for different purposes have tended to be provided independently of each other by the donors. A reduction in the need for food aid did not mean that other types of aid would increase correspondingly. In fact commitments of aid varied greatly from year to year as may be seen from the Table 3.1. The provision of food was vital, and the money value of food aid trebled between 1973–4 and 1974–5. The price of wheat had risen rapidly as a world shortage of it became apparent, while at the same time Bangladesh needed even more of wheat from overseas when calamitous floods in 1974 destroyed part of the harvest. The large rise in non-project aid between 1973–4 and 1974–5 similarly reflected the increased cost of imports affected by escalation in the price of oil and world inflation. Much of the project aid committed up to 1973 was for the re-activation of projects started before independence. It was easy to sign accords for this: it was another matter to reach agreement about new developments and programmes to be formulated and negotiated from scratch.

TABLE 3.1 Commitments of aid, 1971–2 to 1977–8, in US$ million

	1971–2	*1972–3*	*1973–4*	*1974–5*	*1975–6*	*1976–7*	*1977–8*
Food aid	157	272	149	457	257	130	133
Non-project aid	271	339	186	419	355	289	388
Project aid	199	330	219	406	318	238	614
TOTALS	627	941	554	1282	930	657	1135

SOURCE: *Seven Years of External Assistance to Bangladesh*, Ministry of Planning, Dacca, June 1978.

The total of aid committed has fluctuated from year to year but there can be little doubt that it has been on an ascending scale. Donors seem to have recognised, as has Bangladesh herself, that very large amounts of aid will need to be committed if Bangladesh is ever to develop its economy effectively.

The diversity of sources of aid to Bangladesh is considerable.

For food, the United States and Canada continue to be major donors but the United Nations, under its World Food Programme, and the EEC have also contributed substantially. For non-project aid which has accounted for some 30–40 per cent of the total, the World Bank is the most important source, followed by the United States and Canada. The Federal Republic of Germany and Japan have also contributed, and the commitment of some $60 million of non-project assistance by Japan in 1977–8 may represent a very significant recent change in the pattern of allotment of aid. Project aid has increased from small beginnings and amounted to over $600 million in 1977–8; more than half the total assistance provided.

It is the Western countries acting either individually or through the World Bank or other international organisations, who are the main providers of aid to Bangladesh. With the establishment of a consortium of donors in 1974, the provision of aid from these sources formally takes on a certain collective element; in 1977–8 commitments from this source amounted to almost 90 per cent of the total, the remainder coming in roughly equal shares from socialist countries and those of the Organisation of Petroleum Exporting Countries (OPEC). Changes in the pattern of sources of aid may reflect shifts in economic and political alignments and socialist countries and those of the Organisation of Petroleum centrally planned economies of Europe fell from 20 per cent in 1973–4 to 5 per cent in 1974–5 and to a mere 1 per cent in 1977–8 and, contrary to the increase in assistance from other sources, has shown no sign of rising again. The total amount of aid provided by socialist countries is, in any case small. Characteristically, the centrally planned economies have provided project rather than non-project aid.[4] What commodity aid was given by the East European countries to Bangladesh tended to consist mainly of equipment, components and spares rather than industrial raw materials and intermediate goods. Out of a total of about $400 million of aid committed to Bangladesh by the centrally planned economies during the years 1972–5, three-quarters was in the form of project assistance. If Bangladesh had been dependent on the socialist countries for supplies of food and raw materials, she would have fared very badly; only 5 per cent of such aid came from them. On the other hand, they contributed by more than one-quarter of all project aid committed. In this respect sources of aid were complementary.

Over the period December 1971 to mid-1978, only 7 per cent of the assistance provided by centrally planned economies was in the form of grants, whereas nearly half of the much larger total amount of assistance received from other donor countries, whether developed market economies, OPEC countries or impoverished India, was free. The distribution of total grants and loans according to source is given in Table 3.2.

TABLE 3.2 Percentage distribution by source of grants and loans: December 1971 to June 1978

	Grants	*Loans*
Developed market economies	60	47
Oil-producing countries, India and Pakistan	12	9
Centrally planned economies	1	12
Multilateral agencies	27	32
TOTALS	100	100

SOURCE: *Seven Years of External Assistance to Bangladesh*, Ministry of Planning, Dacca, June 1978.

The preference of different types of donors for particular projects is one of the subjects discussed in a later chapter. It was an important factor in trying to match the needs of Bangladesh with the potentialities of individual donors. Developed market economy countries spread their aid fairly widely with a particular emphasis on non-project aid and on the agriculture and water sector. Oil producing countries and India concentrated project aid on the industrial sector; the non-project aid they offered was used for social and economic infrastructure. The centrally planned economies concentrated on physical as well as social and economic infrastructure. Multilateral agencies concentrated on agricultural development and contributed inputs needed to keep industry going. This mainly reflected the interest of the World Bank in rural development and the recognition that means had to be found to increase the flow of raw materials and other inputs.

In times of dire need it is important to utilise aid quickly. There is always a time lag between the commitment of aid and its utilisation, which for project aid, may extend over years taken up with project preparation and construction. The same constraints do not apply in the case of food and commodity aid, although some time is likely to elapse before orders are placed and transportation accomplished, which can be greatly extended if there are administrative bottlenecks. Table 3.3 is designed to give a general impression of the different rates of disbursement characteristic of different forms of assistance and to show how this has changed over a given period; it needs, however, to be interpreted with some care.

TABLE 3.3 Availability and disbursement of aid, 1971–2 to 1976–7 (amounts in US$ million; ratios in percentages)

	Project aid	*Non-project aid*	*Food aid*	*Total aid*
1971–2				
Availability (A)	199	271	157	627
Disbursement (D)	7	123	113	244
Ratio of (D) to (A)	3	45	72	39
1972–3				
Availability	522	486	316	1325
Disbursement	84	291	183	559
Ratio of D to A	16	60	58	42
1973–4				
Availability	657	381	282	1230
Disbursement	138	109	233	480
Ratio of D to A	21	29	83	36
1974–5				
Availability	925	691	507	2122
Disbursement	145	399	375	919
Ratio of D to A	15	58	74	43
1975–6				
Availability	1099	647	389	2135
Disbursement	129	378	306	813
Ratio of D to A	12	58	78	38
1976–7				
Availability	1208	558	213	1979
Disbursement	147	249	106	502
Ratio of D to A	12	45	50	25

SOURCE: *Seven Years of External Assistance to Bangladesh*, Ministry of Planning, Dacca, June 1978.

NOTE: Availability includes aid in the pipeline at the beginning of the year as well as new commitments during the year.

The outstanding feature is the very slow rate of utilisation of project aid. Although project aid of considerable magnitude has been committed to Bangladesh every year, the amount waiting in the pipeline had increased to well over US$ 1000 million in 1977. Actual disbursement remains sluggish at US$ 150 million a year and, measured in real terms, appears to have declined. Judging by the table it takes six or seven years on the average to utilise project aid in Bangladesh as in many other less-developed countries. The effect of this is that the time at which Bangladesh benefits from aid depends to a great extent on the form the commitments take. The very large commitment to Bangladesh of over $600 million of project aid in 1977–8 shown in Table 3.1 will not on past showing give much benefit to the economy until 1985 or later. It may, of course, be possible to increase the rate of disbursement but with the current swing towards rural development projects with long gestation periods this will prove very difficult.

Non-project aid has been utilised much more rapidly and it may seem with some measure of increasing efficiency. Even so, a period of one to two years appears to elapse between the commitment of aid and its utilisation. For food aid, it should be noted that commitments are frequently made towards the end of a financial year and that such aid is intended to some extent to assist the establishment of reserve stocks; in any event the rate of utilisation of food aid has been rather good.

In conclusion, it may be said that all appearances are that Bangladesh is now firmly set on a programme of economic management and development that involves heavy dependence on aid, most of which must be expected to be provided by consortium countries. The die is cast and with it all the interrelationships that exist between those that give and those that receive will come into play and will continue to dominate both the domestic scene in Bangladesh and its foreign relations policy. It would be wrong to think that aid relations can work without friction. Yet, they are capable of being improved on both sides in the future, as they have been hitherto in some respects. This will require a better insight into the nature of these relationships and of the constraints and opportunities for such accommodation. This is really the reason for writing about the experience of aid and influence in Bangladesh.

Notes

1. See, for example, *The First Five Year Plan, 1973–78*, Planning Commission, Government of the People's Republic of Bangladesh, Dacca, November 1973, and A. R. Khan, *The Economy of Bangladesh*, Macmillan, London, 1972. Other references are given in footnote on p. 13.
2. The classifications do not entirely correspond and some estimates have had to be made, but discrepancies are unlikely to disturb the general conclusions. Figures of imports by category are given in the (draft) Two-Year Plan for 1978–80, p. 20.
3. Continued reliance on aid to finance public development expenditure seems to be assumed in the draft plan for the two years 1978–80; only a small reduction in previous levels is proposed.
4. To some extent this is also true of China which started to give aid in 1976, it has, however, also provided some commodity assistance to Bangladesh.

Part Two:

Relationships to Donors

4 Aid Requirements and Donor Preferences

NURUL ISLAM

It is sometimes assumed that putting an aid programme together is a mechanical business involving no more than the exercise of a little arithmetic. Nothing could be further from the truth. Even the arithmetic is not easy, for it depends on many assumptions of dubious validity; while matching the amount of aid that might be required, both in total and in its components, to that which might be on offer is a multi-dimensional problem of great complexity, not least in its political aspects. All aspects of the problem interact and it is not possible to say logically that one can be solved ahead of the others; the solution is essentially interactive by nature. It is only for the convenience of exposition that we examine the procedures adopted for the formulation of aid requirements first and follow this with a discussion of the problems involved in matching aid requirements to the readiness of particular donors to provide assistance in the amounts and forms ultimately determined by them.

The size of the First Five Year Plan was determined only after examining a number of alternatives in some detail. Each of these alternatives had different aid requirements which were assessed with the help of an input-output model of the economy. While the model simplified the calculations involved, as they could be computerised, it could do nothing to relieve planners and other policy makers of the task of determining the preferred composition of alternative programmes. Also, the work of the planners and the usefulness of the model they used were dependent on the data available, which in many cases was of indifferent quality. So far as aid requirements were concerned, a basic purpose of all such calculations was to calculate the investment needs of the economy in relation to given objectives and to deduct from this total the amount that could be financed by domestic savings; the difference was assumed to represent external financing needs. As we have indicated, this was not to be regarded as an end product but as a starting point for further calculation and as a basis on which discussions could be started with donors.[1]

There was simply no means of telling how much aid would be forthcoming over a five year plan period, particularly at a time when new aid relationships were in the course of being established and when unresolved issues between Bangladesh and her suppliers clouded the future outlook. There were also many uncertainties about how available aid could be used. Moreover, individual donors often wish to finance particular projects and may, or may not, be prepared to provide general balance of payments support. Such national preferences do not always coincide with the needs of the recipient country. Finally, there may be also, as we shall see, problems of reconciling the availability of aid with the views of ministries and other public bodies on the sources of support they prefer. All these problems had to be resolved in the course of aid discussions.

Formulation of Aid Requirements

The Bangladesh First Five Year Plan for 1973–8 provided a general framework and gave direction to the economy. The implementation of the Plan was guided by annual plans and annual development programmes, in which specific aid requirements were estimated in detail. The simultaneous preparation of the domestic budget, the foreign exchange budget and the annual plan was designed to ensure that the estimate of foreign assistance needed was consistent with the projected balance of resources, including the savings gap.

The annual development programme consisted of a list of projects on which expenditure would be incurred during the year. Most of the projects included in the list for any year, had already been begun and were part of an on-going programme; others were intended to be started during the year, subject, in some cases, to the completion of feasibility studies. Often the inclusion of a new project depended on whether external financial support for it could be found. Where donors had expressed interest in such a project, financial provision might be made for it in the annual programme, even though it would often be necessary to carry out detailed feasibility studies before aid could be committed. Thus the annual development programme itself and its estimates of foreign aid requirements were, in some measure, tentative.

For all projects the annual plan indicated the total expenditure that it was expected would be incurred; it also divided this into foreign exchange and domestic components. Details about the time that was expected to elapse before the project was completed and the annual phasing of both domestic and foreign exchange expenditure were included in a prescribed project report; this report had to be approved by the Cabinet with the implication that the need for continuing support in the future was accepted. The foreign exchange component of expenditure on an approved project did not necessarily correspond exactly with the amount of foreign assistance assumed for it. In some cases, foreign expenditure might be financed in part through commodity aid or from Bangladesh's own foreign exchange resources; in others, the amount of project aid available might exceed the estimated foreign exchange outlay on the project, because of the inclusion of foreign assistance intended for the finance of local expenditure.

The foreign exchange budget devised for the year in the annual plan had to take account of all sources of foreign exchange and all purposes for which it was needed. This was a complicated operation. Requirements of foreign exchange had to be carefully matched with the sources from which it could be obtained. It was necessary to present a comprehensive picture each year of how projected expenditures were to be met and to revise this during the year when circumstances changed, as they often did. All this involved the preparation of comprehensive import programmes. An important element in making needs and resources meet and tie was the availability of foreign exchange directly under Bangladesh's own control, without restriction of use. Since export receipts were small in relation to total needs, and project and food aid by their nature were not available for general balance of payments support, drawings on the IMF and grants and loans for general purposes provided an invaluable element of flexibility in designing import programmes. Among other things, such 'free' foreign exchange had to be used for debt service and payments for invisibles that could not be accommodated in aid programmes.

In addition to operating as an administrative device for the apportionment of imports, the annual foreign exchange budget provided a basis for negotiation with donors about future needs for commodity and project assistance. In all aid negotiations forward planning of foreign exchange was the basis on which aid requirements could be assessed and presented in a comprehensive framework for donors.

The Process of Aid Negotiation

The comprehensive framework in which aid requirements were articulated set the stage for a response by donors, but request and response did not follow in a clear cut time sequence. The dialogue was continuous; requests were formulated and responses received, some favourable, others not; discussions and negotiations were often protracted. There were several stages, from preliminary to final, in which requests for assistance were made. When it came to giving a foreign assistance agreement its final form, the donors were often closely involved in determining what was needed and what should be the mechanics and procedures of project implementation; it was necessary for Bangladesh to meet general and detailed donor standards and criteria, elaborated and agreed in the course of the preliminary discussions.

Much the same process of continuous interchange was evident in aid discussion with groups of donors. From the formation of the aid group in 1974,[2] a formal document was prepared for members; this indicated the broad outlines of the aid required; its quantum and major components spelt out in terms of commodities, project assistance and food aid. The background to these requirements lay in an analysis of the shortage of resources available for investment as well as the need for foreign resources. Most of the ideas and figures which were presented in the document submitted to the meeting of the consortium, had already been the subject of earlier preliminary discussions not only with the representatives of the World Bank (the organiser of the consortium) but also with major bilateral donors.

While this was going on the donors gave preliminary indications of the amount and nature of assistance which they had in mind. A few of them, notably the Netherlands and the Scandinavian countries, had the practice of providing an indication each year of the quantum of assistance that Bangladesh could expect to receive from them in the next two to four years. Even though the amount of aid from these sources was not a large proportion of the total, it helped in the process of estimating the volume of foreign aid which might be available beyond the immediate future. The larger donors were much less precise in forecasting the aid they might make available, but in consortium meetings they did provide 'indicative' figures at least for the immediate future. Frequently, this was no more than a formalisation of indications that had previously been given in bilateral discussions.[3] Such indicative figures were treated as being minimum amounts of aid commitments with the expectation that actual availability of aid would be somewhat larger. For those countries which gave no indications of future levels of aid, the amount given in previous years was taken as a starting point for negotiating aid for the following year.

Discussions with donors often identified projects and commodity assistance that would be likely to attract support. In some cases, the amount of aid under consideration was based on preliminary cost estimates, which might be modified subsequently. A great deal of uncertainty often remained, and was most important in the case of the US, where aid commitments were subject to changes in the political climate and varying modes of congressional approval.

As Bangladesh progressively identified its detailed requirements of commodity aid and project assistance, donors found they had more and better formulated options available bearing on the kind of assistance they might provide, whether they would wish to concentrate on commodity aid, or on project aid, or be willing to finance both in some proportion. The Planning Commission tried to arrange its programmes in conformity with the special preferences of donors. The final determination of what was to be financed often depended on whether suitable projects could be found and their costs and benefits evaluated. Although donors frequently indicated how they preferred their aid to be used, they might be prepared to modify their views in response to requests by Bangladesh during negotiation. Others, more accommodating, would invite suggestions from Bangladesh and after studying them would make their choice from the list of projects submitted.

In respect of development assistance from the centrally planned economies the process of aid negotiation was somewhat different. Mostly, they provided project assistance and loans to finance supplies of components and equipment. A list of projects was frequently submitted by them; often these served to indicate their preferences among items included in a corresponding list submitted by Bangladesh. On the whole they left it to Bangladesh to choose which of the projects, suggested by them, were suitable for Bangladesh. While for the USSR and most countries of Eastern Europe negotiations about development assistance took place between governments on both sides, in the case of Yugoslavia discussions and agreements were conducted with their decentralized enterprises, since there was no central agency responsible for such matters.

There was considerable interest and expectation in Bangladesh in the early period of its independence with respect to development co-operation with the USSR. In mid-1972, during the visit of an economic delegation from the USSR, the Government of Bangladesh, following its practice with other donors, submitted its initial proposals for assistance from the USSR, covering projects, equipment and raw materials, all to be financed by credit. The list of equipment extended from construction machinery, tugs, ferries and steamers to X-ray and surgical equipment. The list of raw materials included raw cotton and cotton yarn, pig iron and steel products, crude oil and petroleum products, edible oil and chemicals. The Soviet Delegation responded by referring the list of raw materials to separate consideration for inclusion in trade agreements, but was ready to examine the other two lists. Members asked questions about technical details of projects and indicated tentative interest in some, while declining to pursue others. It transpired from the discussions about the list of equipment and machinery, that a long lead time was dictated by the nature of Soviet planning. Most of the supplies to be furnished under credit, whether complete plants or pieces of equipment and machinery, had to be fitted into the production plans of the individual enterprises. The production targets laid down for economic sectors and for enterprises within each sector were set as far ahead as five years, although variations within limits could be made from year to year. The commitment of supplies for export, as well as the supply of imports, was programmed as part of highly centralised and inflexible five year or annual plans, which rendered it difficult or impossible to supply goods 'off the shelf'. Inventories were small, and it was necessary for those receiving credits to indicate their requirements well in advance so that Soviet enterprises could integrate them in their production plans. Sales made under overseas credit arrangements and those made in the domestic market could not be interchanged; there was no market mechanism to facilitate this in the way that is open to Western donors in many instances.

Donors' Sectoral Interests and Special Competence

Missions to analyse and appraise the economic situation and prospects of Bangladesh were sent by a number of countries. They would have discussions with the Planning Commission as well as with the administrative ministries. Such discussions often covered the entire range of Bangladesh's economic problems, prospects, priorities and patterns of development and the pursuit of economic policies consistent with objectives and priorities. Sometimes such visitations were concerned with studying particular sectors in depth, often with a view to identifying projects that a country could support. Identification of projects by general or sector missions would be followed by visits from specialists designed to appraise in depth the suitability of specific projects for support. Each economic sector had its unique problems of project identification and implementation.

The sectoral pattern of assistance given by countries and agencies before the liberation of Bangladesh tended to be carried over. This was due partly to inertia and partly to a feeling that past experience in these sectors, would ensure success in the future. Donors as well as Bangladesh herself had developed expertise in particular sectors; what they had learned from past experience in implementing projects in a certain sector gave them the confidence derived from dealing with the familiar.

Project assistance was more often than not associated with technical assistance.[4] The technical experts from a given donor country or agency working in a particular sector tended to develop a vested interest in that sector, and to establish an identity of interest and a close working relationship with the development agencies of the recipient. Technical assistance was a powerful force making for continued activity in given sectors even when it was not supplied in connection with particular projects. The technical assistance provided by Canada for the railway, by the Dutch for airways and by the UK for industry led to other requests for project assistance from these countries as recognised sources of technical expertise in their respective fields.

The types of projects undertaken by donors in Bangladesh were often those they supported in other countries as well. They tended to choose sectors in which they had experience, the assumption being that good ideas that worked elsewhere could be repeated and previous mistakes avoided. The problems in transferring technology from an industrialised country to a developing country are many and varied; it may well be helpful for a given donor country or agency to concentrate on a limited number of fields. Experience with, say, fertiliser plants or electric power plants in a wide variety of developing countries gives an opportunity to build up expertise and apply it with assurance in different situations.

Some donor countries are generally recognised for their technology and experience in the production of capital equipment for particular uses. Not surprisingly, they tend to favour (within their special range of competence) those sectors or subsectors in which they have excess capacity in the supply of capital equipment. Thus, it was not unusual to find that the composition of a given country's project assistance reflected domestic pressures to ensure export orders for those enterprises and industrial sectors which needed it most, often as a matter of political necessity.

All these considerations were reflected in varying degrees in the projects selected for assistance by donor countries and agencies. Bangladesh for its part, tried to distribute its projects among the various donors in accordance with what it conceived to be their respective comparative advantage or reputation in various fields, as revealed either by its own experience with aid projects in the past or by the general reputation of the country in particular sectors. The centrally planned economies provide illustrations of this. They had a great deal of experience in the generation, transmission and distribution of power in developing countries as well as in their domestic economies; they naturally emphasised this capability, as well as their proficiency in heavy industry.

Bangladesh therefore tended to submit power projects to these countries, knowing that they looked on them with more favour than projects in other sectors.

There was no guarantee that any project submitted to a particular country would qualify for assistance and it made sense to try to interest more than one donor at a time. To have waited for a refusal before trying an alternative source of assistance would have led to inordinate delays in project negotiation. Each donor country inevitably took a long time to complete negotiation on a major project and a time lag of two years before a project was accepted or rejected was quite normal. This practice of parallel negotiation was not without its embarrassments; two or more countries might become interested in a project, but only one could be invited to carry it out.

The centrally planned countries, expert though they were in the provision of power projects, were not alone in having relevant experience in Bangladesh in past years; others were Canada, the United Kingdom and the United States. The only existing hydroelectric power project in Bangladesh had been financed by The United States Agency for International Development (USAID); and since a proposal to construct a further power unit in the same project had been agreed with the US before liberation this was an obvious project to take up again with the same donor. Similarly, the Asian Development Bank (ADB) was already involved in a project for power generation. Bangladesh decided to approach simultaneously all these sources of support to ascertain their readiness to provide assistance in the power sector.[5] The comparative advantage of the centrally planned economies lay in providing infrastructure and heavy industry as they had done in India, Pakistan, Sri Lanka and other countries with success; whether their technical competence was as great as that available in Western countries was beside the point. Thus the Planning Commision allocated a railway project to Hungary, even though the ministry concerned would have preferred it to be financed by Germany, Japan or the UK because there was greater familiarity with equipment from those countries.

Considerations of a different kind could affect the type of project that countries were asked to undertake. Rural development projects, those concerned with health and education, and other projects that required considerable local financing were not presented to the socialist countries; this was partly because

Western countries, unlike the socialist ones, were prepared to finance some local costs (thus providing support for the import programme) as well as to pay for imports needed directly for the projects themselves.

Preferences of Major Donors

The USSR preferred projects in which they had experience elsewhere in the developing world or in other East European countries, and they had a preference for projects producing output which could be exported to the USSR in repayment of their credit. They attached importance to ensuring that the debtor country would build up its repayment capacity and therefore favoured investment in export industries. Under the terms of Bangladesh's credit agreements with the USSR, a large part of repayment was to be in the form of Bangladeshi goods, both traditional and non-traditional exports. For example, while the USSR aid negotiators were willing to give credit for capital equipment and machinery for the textile industry, they were averse to supplying raw cotton and cotton yarn except if this was clearly to be used to produce textile fabrics for export to the USSR. The advantage of this kind of package deal for Bangladesh was that it might raise income and employment; the difficulty was that most of the industrial projects in which Bangladesh was interested were to promote import substitution, such as refining oil, and producing machine tools, steel and petrochemicals; in the few other cases where industrial activities producing goods for export might be developed, the USSR was unlikely to provide a market.

Among donors expressing a preference for financing projects in specific sectors of the economy the US Government was most explicit in stating the main priorities of its aid programme. Prior to independence, USAID had been involved in financing infrastructure with such projects as highways, canals, bridges, and power projects. Post independence, the focus was on agricultural and rural development in general and food production in particular, with emphasis on meeting the nutritional requirements of the majority of the people. Population planning and health, education and human resource development were also high in the list of priorities. In connection with increased food production, USAID was interested in labour intensive irrigation and water control projects, such as coastal embankments, as well as in the promotion of the domestic fertiliser industry.

The British Government, unlike that of the United States, did not start with predetermined views about the areas or sectors they wished to assist, but entered into a prior discussion with the Planning Commission and the ministries concerned. In effect, British assistance covered three areas: agriculture (including water resources), industry, and power and communications. In industry they were interested in the jute and textile industries, which had traditionally purchased capital equipment and machinery from the UK. The same was true of established power and communications installations.

The Government of Japan sent a high powered mission to Bangladesh in 1974. It consisted of representatives of both the public and private sectors and had the task of exploring and selecting areas for economic assistance. The mission members' review was far-ranging and they identified a number of areas for Japanese economic assistance. In agriculture they recommended technical assistance for extension work directed to the introduction of new techniques of production, and the establishment of a model production area in which modern methods of organisation and improved production techniques should be applied, including the use of high yielding seeds combined with a measure of mechanisation. The mission showed great interest in the exploitation of natural gas and the establishment of petrochemical industries based on it, as well as in offshore exploration for petroleum. In the industrial sector they recommended technical assistance in operation and management, and financed supplies of equipment for modernisation and balancing, and the purchase of raw materials and intermediate imports.[6]

The Japanese mission was clearly most interested in projects that might provide resounding evidence of Japanese accomplishments or could serve as a visible symbol of co-operation between Japan and Bangladesh, including hospitals and hotels and, most strikingly, a bridge over the Jamuna. The fact that the bridge would be very expensive and take a long time to complete was apparently not considered to be of great moment: it was thought of as a centrepiece of Japan's development endeavours in Bangladesh. The bridge, which would connect the North and South of the country, would eventually be appreciated by the multitude who would use it; it would, in short, be a monument to Japanese co-operation, a political accomplishment transcending immediate economic considerations of the best use of scarce resources.

As early as 1973 the Japanese Government carried out a feasibility study of the project which, it was suggested at the time, could be constructed in a mere three years. The survey mission, which had recommended and initiated the feasibility study of the bridge under the Japanese technical assistance programme, was able to report that the construction of the bridge was technically feasible; it further justified its recommendation on the ground that the Government repeatedly had accorded special priority to bridge construction in the post-war period. If the economic feasibility of the bridge were to appear less than favourable, the mission suggested, the bridge should also be assessed by the alternative criteria of socio-political considerations and by making allowances for other and wider impacts of the project.

Preferences of Small Donors

Small donors usually preferred to concentrate on one or two project or programme areas in which they had developed special competence, in part because such concentration would make their aid programmes easier to administer and more likely to have a noticeable impact. Often, however, the amount of assistance that these countries could make available was too small for their distinctive contribution to be evident.

New Zealand concentrated on aerial spraying of pesticides on crops and on the construction of a hospital. Special aircraft had been developed for crop spraying by New Zealand and experience had been gained of their use in Indian conditions. The project put forward for Bangladesh provided aircraft, pilots and spare parts and included arrangements for training Bangladesh pilots and supporting staff. The hospital was for crippled and disabled children, and, here again, in addition to providing the building and equipment, assistance in training Bangladesh experts was included as part of the package.

Dutch assistance was initially entirely concentrated on dredgers and aircraft for internal air services. It was not long, however, before aid started to be more diversified, even though there was an unsatisfied need for dredgers built in the Netherlands and provided as part of their aid programme. By 1974, Dutch loan assistance financed the purchase of dredgers, airport telecommunication equipment, inland water tugs, laboratory and research equipment for universities, sugar mills, radio equipment, requirements of small industries and the like. In addition, by 1975 the Dutch showed active interest in rural development projects, including small scale irrigation, drainage and flood protection schemes and the provision of health and social services, thus diversifying their aid programme still further.

Norway, and later on Denmark also, indicated that they would like to concentrate their efforts in such sectors as inland and coastal water transport (including navigational aids, tugs, small vessels and technical education), fishing and agro-based small industries. Assistance had been given in all such sectors in the 1960's and it proved possible in the course of the first two years after independence to identify and agree on a number of projects in all these areas. In addition, a good part, particularly of Norwegian aid, was made available for the finance of commodity imports.

Swedish assistance to Bangladesh was initially given overwhelmingly in the form of commodity assistance, including the provision of second-hand ships urgently requested by Bangladesh. Before independence, Sweden had been involved jointly with the International Development Association of the World Bank (IDA) in providing assistance to technical education and to the agricultural university at Mymensingh, in financing water supply and sewerage projects, gravity and tube-well irrigation, roads and highways, as well as small-scale industries. Most of these projects were unfinished in 1971 and Sweden continued to participate in them after independence. After a while Sweden also showed a growing interest in rural development and agricultural projects. Co-operative credit and marketing projects concerned with agriculture, fishing, forestry, weaving and dairying, and the training of co-operators, therefore assumed increasing importance in negotiations for Swedish aid.

World Bank Preferences

Credits from international organisations were larger in total than assistance from individual countries and so were more widely spread among sectors. The most important multilateral source of economic assistance was the International Development Association of the World Bank. Before independence, project assistance provided by the Bank group to the territorial area of Bangladesh had been divided in roughly equal proportions between agriculture, transportation and industry, urban water supply and telecommunications. The eleven ongoing projects, financed by the World Bank group and reactivated in post-independence Bangladesh, included three irrigation and drainage projects, two urban water and sewerage projects, one each in telecommunications, education, small-scale industry, highways and grain storage, and one major reconstruction project following the cyclone destruction in late 1970. The choice of projects had been mainly determined by the availability of well prepared projects which passed the test of the Bank's cost-benefit analysis.

In the early seventies, and particularly after independence, the Bank gave more attention to rural development projects and to health and populations projects. It explained its inability to do so earlier in the following terms:

> 'the relatively low proportion of lending for agriculture, in a country where over 80 % of the population is directly dependent on agriculture for its livelihood, [was] primarily due to the very unusual difficulties encountered in project preparation. These difficulties result from Bangladesh's particularly difficult environment with a terrain interlaced with rivers, a climate that regularly brings devastating floods as well as droughts, and with a very high population density'.[7]

To seek to deal with these difficulties, the Bank took a number of new initiatives to try to shift the emphasis of aid. The Bank completed a massive study on water and land use in Bangladesh before independence (the so-called Nine Volume study, there were ten actually). It was a far ranging and comprehensive survey, yet it was no more than a preliminary analysis and guide to the strategy that might be followed, clearing the ground for decisions within the Bank about the types of projects to prepare. In addition, the Bank initiated a number of studies of specific sectors: a major study of jute production and manufacturing, another of the potentiality for non-jute exports, and also a study concerned with assistance to small-scale industry. In 1973 Bangladesh accepted an IDA technical assistance credit to finance work on the formulation of projects (including pre-investment planning), feasibility and engineering studies, consulting and advisory services, and the training of Bangladesh staff. All of these initiatives were primarily directed to expedite and improve the formulation of projects suitable for World Bank IDA financing.

Early in 1973 a Bank mission identified a number of potential projects on the basis of the Bank's earlier study of land and water use in Bangladesh, which could qualify, with further preparation, for World Bank assistance.[8] The criteria for the identification of such projects were specified, including the requirement that projects had to be capable of sufficiently rapid preparation to be started within two years; they had to contribute to increased employment and income in rural areas; they had to facilitate grass roots participation and the building up of local institutions; they had to economise in the use of capital and avoid Government commitment to major indivisible capital outlays.[9]

The efforts to shift the Bank's involvement in the direction of rural development notwithstanding, the Bank's interest was not confined to things totally agricultural.[10] It continued to involve itself in the development and operation of industry, including assistance to small-scale industry, and specifically in the potentials of large-scale manufacturing based on the utilisation of natural gas.

Notes

1. For a further discussion of these aspects of the planning process see Nurul Islam, *Development Planning in Bangladesh*, C. Hurst & Co., London, 1977, chapters 4 and 5.
2. See Chapter 8. It should be noted that although the discussion of the pros and cons of establishing an association of donors was discussed in terms of a consortium, the title accorded to it when established was that of 'The Bangladesh Aid Group.' The terminology is unimportant.
3. One of the advantages claimed for the formation of the consortium, or aid group meeting, was that donors would formally indicate their commitment of assistance for the following year.
4. It was estimated by the Planning Commission, which was anxious to restrict the use of technical assistance to the minimum, that over Tk400 million ($50 million at 1973 rates) would have to be spent on technical assistance (including equipment and the training of Bangladesh nationals abroad)

during the First Five Year Plan 1973–8. About half this was expected to be needed to pay for the services of foreign experts and advisers working in Bangladesh for varying periods. The Planning Commission estimates imply that at any time some hundreds of technical advisers could be engaged in such programmes.

5. Similar considerations applied in other fields. Both the Dutch and the Danes were reputed for their expertise in the maintenance and dredging of inland water channels. Both were approached in relation to inland river training and building up a dredging fleet.
6. The Japanese mission also indicated support for population planning in Bangladesh.
7. International Development Association, *Report and Recommendation of the President to the Executive Directors on a proposed credit to the People's Republic of Bangladesh for a Technical Assistance Project*, 11 June 1973, p. 2. Report No. P–1281–BD.
8. International Bank for Reconstruction and Development, *Bangladesh Agriculture and Water Development. The Hard Core Programme 1973/74–1974/75*. 8 February 1973.
9. Ibid., p. 3.
10. The World Bank's involvement in population planning activities are dealt with separately in Chapter 10, which also describes the Bank's role in the planning of a major fertiliser unit.

5 Interest Groups and Aid Conditionality

NURUL ISLAM

It was a major task to draw together all the differing interests and capabilities of donor countries and agencies and weld them into a coherent, balanced and effective development programme. Also within Bangladesh, several groups with different interests were involved and exercised pressure and influence. A wide range of conflicting interests had to be reconciled in the process. Aid had to be found to support the import programme, projects had to be assigned to donors and agreed with them, and ministries and development agencies had to be convinced that they could not always be allowed to arrange things exactly as they wished.

In Bangladesh the Planning Commission was ultimately responsible for setting priorities and negotiating foreign economic assistance. The ministries concerned with operations, however, were responsible for negotiating the details of project design and for the specification of equipment and machinery; they were also responsible for the administrative arrangements involved in the implementation of projects and for implementation itself. Their opposite numbers were the agencies administering aid, sometimes international agencies, often those of donor countries. Both sides might employ consultants to assist with feasibility studies and project appraisal. At an early stage representatives of suppliers of machinery and equipment and of construction firms might become involved. When multilateral aid was under consideration, these might be drawn from any of the countries supporting the international organisations concerned; in the case of bilateral assistance they would be likely to be drawn from the country proffering aid.

A distinction should be drawn between officials concerned with the negotiation of aid agreements and suppliers of aided goods. While aid from Western countries was in most cases made available from official sources, the goods bought with it were generally provided by private traders or producers. These private suppliers operated through their agents in Bangladesh; they had established strong links over a period of time with Bangladesh nationals and companies who acted on their behalf and also with officials in the various ministries and government organisations. Private suppliers got to know the preferences of the purchasing departments in Bangladesh as they, in turn, got to know the specialities of the suppliers. Close working and personal links were often developed by suppliers with aid agencies and these suppliers might claim that they were in a position of being able to influence 'aid-givers'. Such claims were sometimes extended to suggesting that the amount of aid available would be adjusted to meet the kind and quantity of purchases made by the recepient country from particular suppliers. Although officials and politicans were aware that such claims were often bogus, they might be led to conclude, on occasion, that the flow of aid did in fact depend on purchases from particular sources and on the kind of goods purchased. When the Planning Commission declined to give credence to such claims it was liable to be accused, however unjustifiably, of being responsible for declining aid.

The interests of those likely to be engaged in carrying out the project, or advising about it, could not be expected to coincide always with those of Bangladesh, or indeed with those expected to finance the project. There was often the possibility of sharp differences when so many groups were involved in varying capacities. It was no easy task to blend and reconcile different views or to balance different objectives and influences; and when it was done there was no guarantee that a compromise solution would be the best either from the point of view of those providing aid or from that of Bangladesh. Ideally 'tied aid' needed to be matched to the comparative advantage of donors in furnishing it, but the pressures of all those concerned in negotiating each agreement might mean that the final result was far removed from this ideal. The resources furnished by aid might have been used more efficiently if an alternative matching of projects to donor capabilities had been possible.

The way in which aid given by particular donor countries was distributed between projects was a matter for the Planning

Commission. The operating ministries were consulted but they could not veto the Commission's decisions, which were not always to their liking. They did, however, seek to exercise their influence by attempting to alter priorities within their respective sectors, and were often successful in ensuring that particular suppliers of their choice were selected for the projects for which they had the responsibility of development. The Ministry of Power and the Power Development Board, for example, greatly preferred to have Western donors, such as the UK, Canada and West Germany as suppliers, while the Telecommunication Department had a preference for West Germany, Holland and the USA, and the Ministry of Transport and Communications and the Railway Board promoted British and West German suppliers. This presented less of a problem than might be expected as most of the suppliers were international combines operating in a number of Western donor countries.

Most of such preferences could be attributed to past experience and association with suppliers in particular countries. Bangladesh's own technical personnel and engineers were familiar with the machinery and equipment of the countries in which they had been trained. They felt confident that they could repair, maintain and operate familiar types of equipment and disliked the thought of having to adapt to new sources of supply. In some cases, when retraining costs were considerable and the changeover would increase the diversity of stocks of components and spare parts, there would have been real costs of departing from traditional sources. Availability of spare parts is always difficult to ensure and it is vastly more serious in countries remote from suppliers. In less developed countries, spares can be produced domestically once local workshops acquire the know-how gained from familiarity with the product. When successful, this provides an insurance against disruption of trade and difficulties of obtaining spares in an emergency. Frequent changes in models and sources of supply make local provision much more difficult.

In a few cases, the preference for continuing with particular sources of supply was due not so much to inertia, lethargy and resistance to adjustments and new technology, as to the possibilities of 'private gain' from purchasing from one source rather than another. Local agents were naturally always concerned to promote the products of their suppliers, and were strongly tempted to offer inducements to those concerned with the placing of contracts in order to get their way. There was a general impression that the indentors and suppliers' agents exercised considerable pressure and influence on the placing of contracts. However, by the very nature of such actions, the extent to which they succeeded in influencing the decisions of the administrative agencies in Bangladesh in favour of one or another source of finance and supply cannot be authoritatively ascertained.

A few instances may be recorded to illustrate the interplay of various interest groups in the allocation of aid between projects and between countries. It must not be inferred that such instances pervaded all sectors of the economy, nor that they necessarily reflect the balance of relative importance of the pulls and pressures of interest groups; they merely demonstrate that they exist.

The instances recorded also show how donors seek to include exportable surpluses, not easily marketable abroad through ordinary commercial channels, in their aid programmes, and illustrate other connections between aid allocations and export promotion. However the special stories reported here, should not be construed to imply that in most cases aid to Bangladesh did not involve a significant contribution from donor countries. But the real cost to the donor country involved in forgoing the use of commodities allocated under aid, either at home or for direct sale in export markets, was often much less than the monetary value of aid accorded. Similarly, when commodities were in great demand at home and prices rising, restrictions were often imposed on exports under aid programmes, the most significant example of this was an embargo on exports of food, fertiliser, edible oil, tallow and the like during 1973–4. In these respects, Bangladesh's experience was not surprising or unique: one of the arguments always used to convince politicians and the public of the desirability of assisting developing countries is that it provides an outlet for the products of the export industries; in short, aid may be regarded as an export credit on favourable terms or even an export subsidy.

Satellite Telecommunications Project

This project was financed by Canada. Negotiations for it were completed before liberation with the Canadian International Development Agency (CIDA) and with RCA Ltd., Canada, the suppliers, who had received 85 per cent of the cost as determined before liberation. A large part of the equipment and machinery needed had been purchased by RCA Ltd., Canada from different parts of the world. It had not been delivered to Bangladesh before independence and was in fact lying in stores in various places, including Pakistan. After independence, it was evident that the equipment needed some adjustment to meet changes in technology in the intervening period and that additional equipment would have to be incorporated. According to RCA Ltd., Canada the cost of the total project had by then escalated to US$ 10 million from the US$ 5.7 million originally estimated. For Bangladesh this raised a number of questions. Was the project worthwhile in view of the substantial increase in cost and the requirements in other sectors? There was an urgent need for essential basic commodities for relief and reconstruction and the escalation in the cost of the telecommunications project would have to be financed at least in part by pre-emption of Canadian aid. The Planning Commission judged that the project could not be justified in the face of competitive needs of higher priority. Moreover, even on the basis of the original capital cost, the yield of the project was very low; at a higher capital cost, losses seemed inevitable. Another aspect of the matter was that the Ministry responsible for advising on the project thought the pace of technical change had been such that more modern equipment could be purchased at about one-third of the revised capital cost estimated for the project equipment when provided as tied aid through RCA Ltd., Canada. Such considerations led the Planning Commision to reject the proposal to use Canadian development loans to defray the increase in cost; alternative demands on this source of finance were more pressing.

No internal costs had been incurred in connection with the project before independence, and Bangladesh considered herself to be under no obligation in respect of Canadian expenditures on projects approved by Pakistan which had not resulted in the installation of capital equipment in Bangladesh; there was no legal or economic case for doing so. Nevertheless, the Planning Commission's decision not to proceed with the project could not be sustained; in the end other pressures prevailed.

The Ministry of Transport and Communication was interested

in the project and wished to see it carried out and argued the case for it within the Government. RCA Ltd., Canada, for its part, eventually succeeded in persuading the Canadian Government to offer the additional amount of money needed to complete the project in the form of a grant. Pressure from the operative ministry, the great interest shown by RCA Ltd., Canada, and the insistence by CIDA that there was no prospect that the additional grant of US$4.3 million needed to complete the project would be available for any other purpose (although in Bangladesh's view there were many projects of higher priority), eventually swayed the decision in favour of the project.

Airways and the Civil Aviation Project

None of the aircraft owned by Pakistan International Airlines was left in Bangladesh for the new airline, Bangladesh Biman, to inherit. The USSR offered to provide planes, spare parts and crews to get the airline going, also to establish training facilities for engineers and pilots as part of a package deal. There was severe resistance to this offer from the airline and the ministry concerned, primarily because the engineers and pilots of Bangladesh Biman were familiar with, and were trained to fly and maintain, Fokker Friendship (Dutch) planes. Retraining would have been necessary before they could operate Soviet planes. It was also true that the Dutch planes were well suited for the conditions in Bangladesh. The Ministry pressed for the purchase of Dutch planes to be financed from the Dutch grant. The Planning Commission, however, felt that the limited amount of Dutch grant available (about six million guilders) would be better used to meet the pressing need for dredging equipment, both for the ordinary maintenance of waterways (which become silted each year with the monsoon and flow of flood water) and to reduce the backlog of work of dredging dead and dying rivers which had been so neglected as to aggravate seriously the risk of flooding during the monsoon.

For a time, what was thought to be an alternative offer of a grant for the purchase of STOL planes from West Germany, was seriously considered. The Bangladesh agent of the West German suppliers of STOL planes informed the Prime Minister, directly and without the knowledge of the Planning Commission and the

Ministry, that STOL planes would be available as a grant from the West German Government, and implied that this grant would be provided as an additional amount over and above that already provided by West Germany for relief and rehabilitation. Subsequently a letter of intent to the West German manufacturing company was issued by the Prime Minister's office, which at that time handled part of relief and rehabilitation aid.

When the Planning Commission had the opportunity to examine the proposal to buy the West German planes it took on a different appearance. STOL planes made in Canada, but of the same type as those it was proposed to purchase from West Germany, had been used in East Pakistan for short hauls, and found not to be very suitable technically under conditions in Bangladesh. Also on economic grounds there was very little to be said for purchasing them in 1972. Moreover, enquiry confirmed that there was no possibility of obtaining an additional West German grant for the purchase of the planes; every plane bought would mean less assistance for reconstruction and rehabilitation. It soon emerged that the West German aid agency itself was against the purchase.

Eventually the proposal was dropped. It was hard to think how it could ever have been seriously considered. The initiative may have been taken by the West German company and its agent in Bangladesh to create a market for planes that otherwise could not have been disposed of. Also the agent may have been led to believe by his West German principals that additional aid would be forthcoming for the purchase of the planes, which would, of course, have been a powerful argument likely to convince Bangladesh of the wisdom of making the purchase in West Germany. Once on the way to making a sale, the agent pressed his advantage hard and argued with the ministry concerned that a rejection of the offer would compromise the office of the Prime Minister, which had issued the letter of intent. In the end this manoeuvering failed and the decision was taken to purchase Fokker aircraft.

The final decision also required the resolution of other issues. It had to be decided how many aircraft should be purchased and when.[1] At the same time, the use of the remaining part of the Dutch credit had to be determined. The need for more aircraft had to be reconciled with the need for dredgers. The Planning Commission felt, on the basis of a survey of requirements for dredgers undertaken by Dutch experts, that the best compromise would be to purchase three dredgers and two aircraft which could be second-hand, together with spare parts. The ministry argued that the aircraft should be new. Finally the Dutch Government decided to increase the amount of its grant in order to make it possible to purchase two new rather than second-hand aircraft in addition to the three dredgers.

The decision to increase the grant can be explained only in part as a simple response to a request from the Bangladesh Government for additional assistance; it may also have reflected commercial pressures in the Netherlands. There had been evidence of similar pressures being exerted when representatives of Dutch manufacturers of railway equipment visited Bangladesh and pressed for the allocation of part of the credit to the railways. The case for such an allocation was that before independence the company had supplied equipment to the railways under a Dutch credit and that unless additional assistance were provided the original equipment would become unserviceable. The ministry responsible for the railways was understandably anxious to continue with the Dutch equipment it was used to; however since it was not confident that it would be able by itself to persuade the Planning Commission to authorise this, it teamed up with its potential suppliers in order to bring pressure to bear. In fact, the Dutch Government had indicated during negotiations that it would be able to respond more favourably to a request which would mean allocation of a part of the credit to the railways, since this would avoid public criticism of favouring aircraft and dredger companies, and only one or two Dutch manufacturers at that.

The decision to purchase two aircraft and three dredgers was not quite the end of the matter. The Ministry of Civil Aviation considered that more aircraft would be needed for Bangladesh Biman to build up its capacity sufficiently to provide services of a standard corresponding to those available in pre-independence days. It therefore insisted on the unusual course of pressing the Planning Commission to earmark the next development loan from the Netherlands for the purchase of two additional new Fokkers. One of the consequences of these decisions was that Danish aid had to be used for the purchase of dredgers, which otherwise might have been built in the Netherlands.

The New International Airport

A new international airport was to be constructed on the outskirts of the capital. The project had been designed before independence by Aeroport de Paris, the French consulting and designing firm, and the runway and framework of buildings had already been largely constructed. A certain amount of equipment from France was specified for incorporation in the project, but the project in its entirety had not been negotiated with any country before independence. When consideration of it was actively resumed in 1975, Aeroport de Paris was again brought in to advise on adjustments necessary in the design of the airport and the additional minimum equipment needed to make it operational in the shortest possible time. The existing Dacca airport had been damaged during the war but temporary repairs had been carried out to make it operational until it was expected to be phased out in 1977.

The immediate problem was to find a source of finance as well as a construction company which would make the new airport operational in two years at an acceptable cost. The longer-term need was to study the effects of the changed volume and pattern of air traffic consequent on the break up of Pakistan on future needs. By far the greater portion of long distance traffic by jet aircraft before 1972 took place between the two parts of Pakistan; this was no longer relevant, and the original long-term master plan prepared before liberation needed to be remodelled. The French consulting and designing firm was engaged to make recommendations about the short-term aspect of making the airport operational. At the same time, a technical assistance team from the Netherlands was engaged in examining and revising the master plan in the new context.

The Ministry of Civil Aviation was anxious to obtain French credit to finance the airport on a turnkey basis. It was not a little disconcerted when the representative of the Philips Company from the Netherlands presented a proposal to undertake the project on a turnkey basis in collaboration with a consortium of Dutch firms and even assured the ministry that the company's influence on the Dutch Government was sufficient to persuade it to allocate a Dutch credit for the project, provided only that the Bangladesh Government would impress the urgency of the project upon the Dutch Government. On further examination, however, it quickly became obvious that the total cost of the project would exceed any reasonably estimated amount of Dutch credit available and that there were a number of other projects already being negotiated with the Dutch Government. The Philips company project could therefore not be financed and completed as proposed within two years without supplementation from other, perhaps French, sources. Further enquiry revealed that the Dutch Minister of Cooperation Development (the aid ministry under the Foreign Office) in fact had had no consultations with Philips on the subject of airport construction in Dacca, and it became evident that the Dutch Government was not willing to allocate assistance for the airport without further scrutiny of the project. In the event, they requested that a report on the short- and long-term economic feasibility of the airport should be prepared by the Dutch technical assistance team which was already engaged in examining the long-term master plan. The Dutch Government made it abundantly clear that Philips could not make any commitment on the part of the Dutch Government. Yet, according to the Bangladesh Ministry of Aviation the company had assured them of their ability to persuade the Dutch Government to use its credit in their favour.

Purchase of Ships under Aid

Bangladesh lost control of all the ships of the Pakistan merchant marine which had previously helped to meet her shipping requirements. Conference and non-conference ships provided a very inadequate and irregular service to Bangladesh ports, seriously hampered the recovery of foreign trade and interrupted development. A timely and regular flow of imports was vital, and Bangladesh attached great importance to the acquisition of a limited number of ships to be operated under her own control. Builders and exporters of ships abounded in Poland and Yugoslavia in Eastern Europe, in the UK, Norway, West Germany and elsewhere in Western Europe, and in Japan: it was to these countries that Bangladesh turned in 1972 in quest of aid in the form of ships. There were two difficulites: first, ships were in great demand at that time, and shipyards were booked for years ahead; second, most countries were unwilling to provide ships under aid programmes. This confirmed the general feeling that mainly export industries with surplus capacity and sluggish demand at home and overseas were to be supported in donor countries through their foreign aid programmes.

Bangladesh made contacts through intermediaries engaged in the sale and purchase of ships, but their principals would sell only for cash. There were other obstacles also. In Japan, traders and manufacturers were willing to supply ships but the aid agency was unwilling to provide finance. Even in Norway, generally very liberally minded about its aid programmes, there was opposition to providing ships under aid, both from shipping interests and from the Government. In the course of negotiations grave doubts were voiced about the ability of Bangladesh to run and manage shipping lines in spite of its well developed connections with the sea. Historically and traditionally the people of Bengal have been a seafaring people. Throughout the days of British rule they provided an important component of the crew of the British merchant service and many worked as crew in foreign ships and others had participated in the management of the Pakistani shipping line. There were in Bangladesh officers formerly with the Pakistan Navy and crew at all levels who, after independence, would not find employment in that capacity, since Bangladesh at the time had no intention of building up a navy of its own. The arguments for providing ships were indeed powerful. While it might have been justifiable to assert that Bangladesh would not have attained a high level of management of its shipping, this was hardly sufficient reason for refusing assistance for an activity which in all probability, and given the willingness to accept technical assistance, would have been able to develop relatively better management than in many other sectors. The refusal by Norway and others at the time to provide assistance for the supply of ships was no doubt determined by the forces of national and sectoral interests in potential donor countries, and not by the merits or otherwise of shipping as a development activity in Bangladesh.

Japanese Relief Grants and Oil Exploration

During 1972 Japan provided Bangladesh with a relief grant, amounting to $12.5 million, which included the supply of textiles. Japanese textile industry representatives visiting Bangladesh frankly asserted that if Bangladesh was interested in getting the kind of textiles of which these suppliers had surplus stocks (samples of which they brought in abundance), the Japanese Government could be persuaded to finance purchases under the grant. Their surplus stock of synthetic fabrics, they pointed out, was due to the loss of a market in the USA, somehow connected with the return of Okinawa from the USA to the control of Japan, as a result of which the Japanese Government was under some obligation to find an outlet for the surplus stocks. A grant to Bangladesh would meet both Bangladesh's dire need for clothing and at the same time get rid of surplus stocks which could not find a market abroad. One problem, however, was that the available surplus stocks did not meet the requirements of wearing apparel in Bangladesh. Synthetic fabrics were unsuitable for all but a small section of the urban population and the quantities on offer were far in excess of the needs of such users. Moreover the fabrics were in a form which could not be easily made into the local traditional dress. There were ready-made garments to dispose of as well, but these also were of no use in Bangladesh. It was explained that the need of Bangladesh was not for synthetic garments but rather for synthetic yarn, which could be woven into appropriate types of fabric for local use and, at the same time, provide employment in the handloom weaving industry. Eventually, as a result of negotiation, part of the grant was split between fabrics and yarn.

Apart from textiles, the grant was available for wagons, tugs and trucks. Bangladesh desperately needed such transport equipment but not in the proportions laid down in the proposed grant. It was not just that Bangladesh had no option to vary the relative numbers of the three items, Japan insisted on fixing the specifications of them as well. In the case of trucks only those carrying about 2.5 tons were available, while 5-ton trucks would have been more useful and economical for carrying food and for other operations in the interior of the country. That the grant offered allowed no room for negotiation, reflected the fact that these special items were being disposed of solely because they were surplus stock; it was evidently felt that as they were available as a grant, Bangladesh should not look a gift horse in the mouth.

Following the oil crisis in 1973, Japan, with her very large dependence on imports of oil from the Middle East, became extremely interested in offshore exploration for oil in the Bay of

Bengal; she was already engaged in the offshore waters of Burma, Malaysia and Indonesia. Politically, Japan had tended to ignore Bangladesh and had participated only to a small extent in the reconstruction and recovery of the country. It was felt that her desire for oil exploration rights in the Bay of Bengal might be used to stimulate her interest and stake in the general development of Bangladesh.[2]

The political interest of the Japanese in Bangladesh might have been aroused if it had been possible to identify a project giving her a commanding interest in the territory of Bangladesh. Such a project might have materialised in the search for oil. Japan wished to undertake a reconnaisance survey of the entire offshore area so that the prospects of finding oil could be ascertained. If this had been carried out, Bangladesh's hand would obviously have been strengthened in negotiating with oil companies in relation to oil exploration contracts. Japan continued to press propositions along these lines for several months but found little favour with Bangladesh. There was at the time considerable disagreement among technical experts on whether it was essential to have a preliminary survey before the entire off-shore area was allocated to different oil companies for exploration. In the end, Bangladesh decided not to have a reconnaissance survey of the entire area.

Politically the pressures were intense and were applied in persistent negotiation. At one stage it appeared that participation in oil exploration, if not in a reconnaissance survey of the entire area, was a *sine qua non* of Japan's readiness to assist Bangladesh. To Bangladesh it began to seem that this would have to be the price to be paid if Japan were to participate in financing a major petrochemical complex; a view that was modified when the petrochemical complex came up for reconsideration. Eventually Japan was given an area for exploration, although it was not the one she had originally hoped to get, and an oil agreement was signed in late 1974. She thus became one of a number of countries involved in exploration for oil in the Bay of Bengal.

Donor Imposed Conditionality

The Western donors, both bilaterally and through multilateral agencies, often sought to go further and attach conditions to projects and programmes financed by them which affected

Bangladesh's ability to run its own affairs and to design and manage its own institutions. In contrast, the centrally planned economies did not generally take it upon themselves to advise Bangladesh about appropriate kinds or lists of projects. Unlike the Western donors, they did not engage in discussions or comments on such matters as the size or priorities of the plan, nor on the policy prescriptions written into them.

All donors tended to involve themselves in the design of the projects. In the case of aid from the West, which was of course the dominant source of assistance, it was the rule rather than the exception for donors to involve themselves with issues such as pricing, management and organisational matters. Programme aid involved discussion of issues relating to import controls and foreign trade and exchange policies, as well as systems of domestic marketing and distribution of imports. These discussions with donors sometimes could be very wide ranging. They went well beyond the issues related to specific projects or programmes or to the problems of the sector in which they fell, to more general issues of development policies and priorities. The presumption that project aid, in comparison with commodity aid, gives rise to a more limited involvement by donors in the discussion of domestic policies and institutions is not necessarily true. It depends upon the nature of the project. Projects in the social sectors, such as health, education and population planning, raise a wide range of questions, because their inter-relations with the entire social framework are complex and closely linked to general policy questions. Discussions on agricultural projects also raise wide issues: the system of village co-operatives, credit extension services, the plight of the landless and small farmers, the pricing policies for jute and rice, and many more besides.

The most trying conditions that were liable to be inserted in agreements for project aid were concerned with management. These conditions generally covered the appointments of foreign consultants and contractors, sometimes also the specific local manager or director to be in charge of the project in Bangladesh. Negotiations on issues of this nature often gave rise to tensions between Bangladesh and the intending donor. While participation by donors in determining the qualifications and duties of a project director was conceded by the Government to be a legitimate involvement on their part, the condition that the appointment of a project director in Bangladesh should be subject to approval of the donors was considered an infringement in the internal administrative affairs of the country. Such cases had to be resolved by negotiation. In one proposal, the donor would have become involved in appointing the administrative head of the Ministry if the Government could have been persuaded to agree to the condition. The issue was resolved by deciding that the qualifications and functions of the person to be appointed would be agreed, leaving the Government free to make a suitable appointment (which turned out well in spite of donor's fears that the contrary would be the case).

The insistence of donors on approving the appointment of a particular person tended to be counter productive. The effectiveness of a person widely known to be the nominee of a foreign aid agency could be impaired by the nature of his appointment. There was also a danger that if he was appointed against the wishes of the Government, he could be rendered ineffective, thus proving to the donors that they were wrong in their choice.

Conditions were frequently laid down in credit agreements relating to the organisational and administrative structure of the project, including the structure of the ministry or agency regulating or controlling the project. For example, a loan for the rehabilitation of the railway included a condition that 'the borrower shall establish . . . the Railway Authority to be responsible for the operation, maintenance and development of railway services within its territories with such powers, responsibilities, management and capital structure, as shall have been agreed between the Borrower and the Bank, and as shall be necessary to enable the Railway Authority to operate as an autonomous commercial-public utility enterprise.'[3] Similar conditions were attached to a loan agreement in the telecommunications sector by the World Bank for the constitution of an autonomous telecommunications board for the management and development of the telecommunication system in Bangladesh. Again, an Asian Development Bank (ADB) loan to the power sector for a 40 MW power station based on natural gas,[4] included a condition for the appointment of a management expert by the Government, in agreement with the donor, who would make recommendations on the organisation and management of the Power Board, which was the agency involved in the regulation and development of the entire power sector of Bangladesh.

The important point to notice in each of these cases is that while the particular loan related to a relatively small project in each of the sub-sectors of the economy and constituted a small fraction of the total sectoral investment or capital assets, the organisational or structural changes enjoined by the donors went much beyond this – to the entire railway sector, or power sector, or telecommunications sub-sector.

In other cases, the composition, powers and functions of the administrative agency were subject to agreement, approval or consultation with the donors. In some instances, the changes in administrative structure and degree of autonomy required by the donors were disliked acutely because it was felt that the financial and administrative autonomy of the national institutions was being abused, and that there would be inadequate authority for supervision and control by ministries on the expenditures and personnel policies and appointments of the country's autonomous agencies. On such occasions the Government questioned the acceptability of the loan in view of the conditions attached to it and yielded only under great pressure.

As might be expected, donors' insistencies were not always regarded as bad by all the various arms of government that became involved. It depended on their point of view. In some such cases donors' requirements could be used by individual ministries to provide supporting arguments and pressures, although such stratagems had to be used with circumspection as there was always the possibility that they would backfire. It was evident that foreigners could exert influence not only because they held the purse strings but also because they were able and ready to try to influence government actions when conflicting interests and views within the government of the receiving country gave them the opportunity. The underlying issue was that the government had to be the ultimate judge of what was good for the country. Aid-givers were welcome to make known the philosophy of their assistance programmes but attempts to administer aid funds or force changes in policies were resented. Such issues might have been avoided if the preferences of donors had been sufficiently explicit and the conditions on which they were prepared to allocate aid stated clearly at the outset. This would have had the added advantage that the principles on which they were operating could have been debated also in their own countries. If this had been done it might have been seen as inappropriate and liable to be harmful, which would have made it more difficult for aid officials, whether the representatives of their own countries, or with greater power, of multilateral organisations, to attempt to intervene strongly in the affairs of aid-receiving countries. Bilateral pressures were more easily resisted as, for example, when aid for the Pabna Irrigation Project was not accepted from the UK because that country desired to place a financial expert on the Water Development Board.

In the case of the establishment of the telecommunications board, the Planning Commission, like the donors, was in favour of a decentralised administrative system with an autonomous professional board. However the Planning Commission was no more capable of ensuring genuine decentralisation than were the donors. Autonomy could not be guaranteed by establishing a formal structure for an organisation if the 'powers that be' were not willing or eager to respect the need for autonomy. Written constitutions granting autonomy to an organisation can be easily violated when frequent changes in legal and institutional structures take place, and in many cases can scarcely be fully observed.

Sometimes aid agreements included conditions designed to ensure the profitability of aided projects, such as specified procedures for the procurement of supplies and management of inventories and stipulations relating to pricing policies. It was not uncommon to attempt to impose conditions relating to domestic project financing, including the capital structure of the projects, and particularly the debt-equity ratio. Such conditions extended to restrictions on the nature and extension of borrowing on the part of the enterprise.

This kind of involvement of donors in financing and pricing policies of aided projects was quite frequent. For example, the Asian Development Bank's loan for a power station based on natural gas, mentioned earlier, required that a financial consultant, appointed by the Government (subject to approval of the Bank), would re-evaluate the assets of the entire power sector, not just those related to the project which was being financed. It was required that the tariff structures would be subject to the recommendations of the financial consultant and that the Government, again in consultation and agreement with the Bank, would reorganise the capital structure of the Power Board. There were also a series of other sweeping and restrictive conditions imposed.[5] It was further stipulated, that the Power Board would formulate and furnish the Bank with a comprehensive programme for adequate rehabilitation and maintenance of the West Zone Power System within twelve months; a clause which seemed to be totally redundant in view of the fact that studies were already being carried out, in collaboration with the Asian Development Bank itself, to see if an interconnection between the Western and Eastern power systems, effectively separated by the Ganges and the Brahmaputra, should be established. Demands for studies often seemed to be asked for as a matter of routine rather than to fulfil a genuine purpose.

Conditions relating to pricing policies were frequently written into project loan agreements, and as a matter of course by the World Bank. The Asian Development Bank followed suit in its loan for rehabilitation of the railway, in which the railway authority was obliged to fix tariffs at a level covering operating expenses and providing a reasonable rate of profit for the capital expenditure programme for the railway system as a whole. It was also required to review its charges to take account of actual and expected changes in the inflation rate, cost increases and financial requirements.[6]

Also in the case of its loan for the development of jute seed, the Asian Development Bank imposed itself into the consideration of wide ranging policy issues extending far beyond the project itself.[7] The project provided for the establishment of jute seed farms under Government ownership and administration, and for strengthening the research effort of the Bangladesh Jute Research Institute through training and provision of consultancy services and other facilities. The Government had to accept the conditions stipulated with respect to the pricing policy to be followed for raw jute and jute seeds, and specific administrative arrangements for implementing an agreed intensive jute cultivation scheme designed to increase the yield per acre. Even though an important part of the project was the development and supply of high yielding seeds, the improvement of jute cultivation would depend for some years to a greater extent on adaptations in cultivation methods, a more intensive use of fertiliser and pesticides and other measures of immediate application. Nevertheless, the Government undertook, as a part of the loan agreement, to take into account any views the Asian Development Bank might offer on the determination of the jute price before it decided the appropriate price, and to inform the Bank forthwith. The Government also undertook to review the price annually in this manner and to announce it at least two months before the beginning of the jute growing season.[8] There were similar provisions in respect of the price of jute seed, seeking both to make its production by growers attractive by high prices, and to make use of it extensively by disposing of the seed at low and subsidised prices.

Although the Ministry of Agriculture was in charge of administering the scheme for intensive jute cultivation, its major preoccupation was achieving increased productivity in rice. Jute tended to be neglected by it. The establishment in 1974 of a Jute Ministry with responsibility for the jute trade was a response to this, but since it had no control over the production of raw jute, the arrangement was scarcely satisfactory. The two ministries failed to co-operate and ill feeling existed between them. In an attempt to overcome this, the Asian Development Bank loan agreement stipulated detailed arrangements for co-operation. These included semi-annual meetings between the two ministries; a December meeting would fix the annual acreage to be covered under the scheme and a July meeting would review achievements and bottlenecks. The arrangements stipulated in the loan agreement to bring the two ministries together could not, of course, solve the basic underlying problem of co-operation, and this attempt by the Bank to impose a solution can at best be characterised as useless.

Notes

1. The second hand aircraft given to Bangladesh by India and Australia to tide her over were due for early replacement and in any case were already out of action for servicing and repair more frequently than normal because of their age.
2. The Ministerial Conference on South East Asian Economic Development, an informal body, under the leadership of Japan, for co-ordinating and stimulating Japanese development assistance, had stopped short of including Bangladesh within the area of membership of the countries of South East Asia. The frontiers of the region, extending from the Philippines in the East, terminated at Burma. Australia and New Zealand, sources of assistance to Bangladesh, had joined the group in 1973–4 as donors. The most important recipient members were Malaysia, Indonesia and Thailand. These countries had accorded a very large role to private enterprise, including liberal concessions to foreign private enterprise, and Japan had significant private investment in them. Burma, which joined in 1974, was an exception. Japan

was not enthusiastic about extending membership of the Ministerial Conference. Bangladesh was not considered a part of South East Asia and if she were included, India could scarcely be excluded. A group, enlarged in this way, would be unwieldy and the additional membership of impoverished countries would dwarf the claims of the original recipient countries on the resources available from Japan.

Japan's interest in oil exploration may have been one response to diplomatic pressure, including US pressure, to involve herself more in giving aid to Bangladesh.

3. Asian Development Bank, *Railway Loan (Loan No 215). Loan Agreement (Special Operations)*, 10 January 1975, p. 9.
4. Asian Development Bank, *Loan Agreement, West Zone Power Project Supplementary*, 23 December 1974, p. 15.
5. Ibid., pp. 15 and 16.
6. Ibid., p. 11.
7. *Loan Agreement (Special Operations) (Jute Seed Project between the People's Republic of Bangladesh and the Asian Development Bank*. Loan no. 213 BAN (SF). 23 December 1974, p. 15.
8. *Loan Agreement (Special Operations) (Jute Seed Project) between the People's Republic of Bangladesh and Asian Development Bank*. Loan no. 213 BAN(SF). *Side Letter No. 4: Project Implementation*. 1974, p. 3.

6 Commodity Aid

NURUL ISLAM

Bangladesh attempted to obtain commodity aid from those countries that had supplied her in the past, irrespective of whether purchases had been paid for out of aid or Bangladesh's own resources. Cotton and iron and steel products had traditionally been bought from the USA and non-ferrous minerals and paper and pulp from Canada and Sweden. It was hoped that these countries would wish to maintain their traditional trading ties and that other countries would wish to do the same. Countries that had financed particular projects in the past might be asked to supply raw materials and spare parts needed to keep them in operation; there was often no alternative source for components and spare parts than the country that had provided machinery in the first place. Commodity aid given by the UK, for example, was used to import spare parts needed by the jute and textile mills originally equipped with machinery from that country. It was also used for replacement parts for the transport system, power plants and electrical transmission and distribution lines.

Most countries, however, preferred to give project rather than commodity assistance. This was a hangover from the prejudices of the sixties on the relative value of project and programme assistance. The former somehow, was thought to promote development and capital formation (regarded as the main focus of development), whereas the latter was assumed to promote consumption rather than capital formation. Old orthodoxies die hard. There were special arguments in favour of commodity assistance in the case of Bangladesh. Spare parts and components were needed in large numbers throughout the economy to make good the damage caused by the war, and stocks needed to be rebuilt to normal working levels. There was also a need to provide raw materials and intermediate inputs previously supplied by

Pakistan which, with the cessation of trade between the two countries, had to be purchased from foreign sources. These requirements had to be met at a time when Bangladesh's exports were severely limited by both supply and demand difficulties. When such adverse factors were compounded by a deterioration in the terms of trade following substantial increases in the price of food, fuel and raw materials, the need for commodity aid was very great indeed.

The case for large amounts of commodity assistance was argued vigorously in bilateral and multilateral negotiations alike. The main sources of commodity assistance were the International Development Association of the World Bank, the United States, the United Kingdom, the Federal Republic of Germany, Canada, Sweden and the Netherlands. Among the socialist countries, the Soviet Union was the only source of non-project assistance, mainly as part of trade agreements. Lists of commodities needed were submitted to various donor agencies or governments; taken together they covered all the requirements for commodity assistance. Many items were included on more than one list, not only because there were alternative sources of supply but also because the requirements of some items were so large that they were unlikely to be met by a single donor. Price was often less of a consideration in deciding between sources of supply than availability. Information on the prices of supplies from various sources was seldom available prior to the negotiation of the commodity lists with each donor. Considerable fluctuation in prices of raw materials and intermediate imports in various markets was a further complication that made comparisons difficult and fluctuations in exchange rates were an aggravating factor. Moreover price quotations applying to ordinary commercial purchases were often found to differ from those quoted once a commodity aid agreement was in operation and purchases were negotiated under it. It was, therefore, a nice piece of judgement to decide what should be included on each list bearing in mind, among other things, that the donor's evaluation of its capacity to supply various items might differ greatly from that of Bangladesh. The lists finally agreed often differed markedly from those originally submitted and it was necessary to insure against such deviations as well as to provide for some choice.

The degree of detail in which the commodity lists were drawn up under commodity aid agreements differed between donors.

The UK and Japan were more exacting in the preparation of lists of commodities needed than were West Germany, Sweden and Canada. Once the broad categories of commodity assistance were agreed with West Germany, it was possible to import any item within the categories laid down and to arrange purchases from suppliers in that country without further negotiation or clearance from the Government. This procedure contrasted with that followed by the UK. The agreement of 1974 provided that commodity aid from the UK could be used for imports for the sectors of agriculture, industry and transport, but it stipulated that such imports should enable existing investments in Bangladesh to be more fully utilised. This required that imports under the UK commodity aid agreement should mainly be composed of raw and semi-finished materials, components and spare parts and small items of capital equipment which were urgently needed for the restoration of the country's economy; such aid could not be used for imports of finished consumer goods. The terms of the agreement might have seemed to be sufficiently clear not to require further interpretation; yet UK aid could not be utilised without clearance for each individual allocation. It was necessary for Bangladesh to provide a full description of each item of imports, to give details of the user of the goods and to furnish information on the volume and estimated cost of the output to be produced; even more inexplicably it was necessary to explain why the UK had been selected as supplier rather than another country. As if this was not enough, Bangladesh was required to supply an analysis in respect of the demand and supply (including stocks) situation in Bangladesh for the item in question and to elaborate this with respect to the arrangements made for storage, distribution, control and maintenance, where appropriate. In the case of each piece of equipment valued at £100,000 or more, a technical and economic assessment of the contribution it was expected to make towards Bangladesh's economic development was also required.[1]

In general, such requests by donors for information, analysis and justification for each item of import conveyed the impression that there was no confidence in the ability or integrity of the recipient to determine its import programme to make the maximum contribution to development. Even so, it was demonstrably unrealistic for the donors to presume that at such great distance they could in fact ensure the objectives they wished to attain by commodity aid. The result was delays and frictions engendered by donor controls. The need to negotiate purchases of almost every individual item more than offset any benefit derived from such cumbersome procedures for the disbursement of commodity assistance.

The Japanese procedures for negotiation and especially disbursement of commodity assistance were particularly complicated. Japan based itself on an extensive analysis of the economy and the import structure of Bangladesh rather than on attempts to justify each individual item of import. Moreover legal and banking procedures for disbursement of Japanese commodity aid were highly cumbersome and time consuming. For a procurement exceeding only 50 million yen (less than US$200,000), it was necessary to provide a description of the items to be procured with a certificate from the suppliers that the items would be supplied and to submit both to the donor agency for its approval before payments could be made to the suppliers. The commodity aid agreement was rigorous in its requirements; it started with a comprehensive description of the commodity aid programme and called for a detailed analysis of the programme, its relation to the Five Year Plan and the expected 'out-turn' of the current economic plan. Information was also requested about changes in the balance of payments and the official gold and foreign exchange reserves during the last five years, as well as the system of foreign exchange and import controls in force.

It may seem scarcely credible that in the case of Japanese commodity assistance, Bangladesh should be asked not only to supply information about the financial and trading institutions through which the commodity loan operated, but also the names and addresses, backgrounds and authorised activities of the members of the board of directors, records of export activities, paid up capital and financial structure, relations with the Government of Bangladesh, organisation of the department or division of the organisation concerned with loan, profit and loss statements, annual reports and the laws relating to the institutions, all of which seemed irrelevant and redundant. A full analysis of the organisation of trading in the private and public sectors had to be supplied together with an analysis of the method of procurement of imports, covering such matters as the system of bidding for import licences, the nature and the description of goods subject to the bidding system, and the method of evaluating and comparing bids. Information was also required about the way in which counterpart funds generated by commodity loans were utilised. Even such rigorous inquiry could not, of course, protect a donor against the non-performance of an insufficient partner.

IDA of the World Bank has been a most important source of commodity aid for Bangladesh. It is instructive to review the purposes and operations of these credits. From November 1972, to the end of 1974, Bangladesh received three commodity loans totalling about $175 million. The first commodity credit, the Reconstruction Imports Credit, was, as its title implied, designed to assist with reconstruction. It was intended to provide equipment and spares to replace or repair capital goods destroyed or damaged in the war, and materials, components and intermediate goods required for agriculture and industry. The list of goods included was wide ranging, covering the needs of transport and communications as well as industry and agriculture.

The second import credit, provided in 1973, had a sharper focus, concentrating on imports for high priority sectors: production for exports, essential consumer goods and requirements in the transportation and construction sectors. The decision to narrow the range of imports permissible under the credit was justified on several grounds: it would enable the Government to meet the needs of the selected sectors in a systematic manner, and it would enable IDA to monitor and supervise the use of credits more efficiently. Another consideration was that items of capital equipment, provided as commodity aid in the first credit, could also be financed under project lending. Since the first credit had been used rather slowly largely because of administrative difficulties, improved procedures were agreed for the second credit which were designed to cut down the time taken to allocate the credit to the agencies that would use it and to speed the issuing of import licences and the opening of letters of credit by the banking system.

The process of negotiating the second import credit started with Bangladesh submitting a list of items for import; this had also been the procedure when the first credit was negotiated, but the information now required was far more demanding and detailed than previously. The list of information required is too long to be conveniently summarised. It included, for example, particulars of the past and proposed use of rock phosphate, details of import requirements of the irrigation programmes carried out by the Bangladesh Agricultural Development Corporation (BADC), particulars of sprayers for crop protection, including inventory figures and requirements, as well as details of machinery needed for the tea gardens. In the industry sector details were required of production, imports and capacity utilisation of industries listed in the credit. For the transport sector information was needed on procurement arrangements and delivery schedules from all sources of buses and trucks and spare parts, as well as details of production and assembly. There were enquiries about the use of the UK line of credit for workshop construction and training facilities for workshop maintenance. Information on pricing policies was called for in respect of all types of transport equipment, including tugs and barges. There were also more general requests for information about the organisation of the distribution system for spare parts and the handling of stocks. A considerable amount of administrative time was taken up in providing such detailed information. Many agencies in Bangladesh questioned whether all of it was really necessary. The information required was not confined to transactions with IDA; it also included enquiries about other sources of finance which had been used in the past year for imports of the type of goods requested, as well as similar information relating to the next eighteen months.

Before the IDA credit could be confirmed and made available for use, the justification for it had to be appraised by a World Bank mission which would recommend how the credit would be apportioned between commodities as well as how much assistance should be made available to Bangladesh. A number of items were deleted from the list of goods submitted by the Government.

Irrigation equipment was excluded, even though it was of high priority, because it was held that it should form part of an irrigation project. The procedure of evaluating the need for project assistance is different from that appropriate for a commodity credit. It involves an assessment of such questions as the optimum location of pumps within the ground water irrigation programme, the efficiency with which equipment could be used relative to its capacity, and the availability of modern inputs, such as fertiliser and high yielding strains of rice, needed to make the best use of supplies of water for irrigation. Such aspects of the irrigation programme could not be evaluated in the course of negotiating a general purpose commodity aid, and IDA considered that it would be assured of a more efficient utilisation of funds if the pumps were provided as part of a project loan. Supervisory requirements were different for project assistance from those prescribed for programme assistance. The Bank wanted the Government to make a thorough analysis of the costs and benefits of different types of irrigation in the light of changes in costs and organisational problems which had emerged in the post independence period. In the course of its negotiation on the Technical Assistance Credit for project preparation, the Bank had identified areas which needed further study in the field of tube-well irrigation, including hydrological surveys and related engineering and economic investigations designed to establish technical and economic feasibilities as well as to determine a potential. Tube-well engineering studies were needed to see whether more economic tube-wells could be designed. There was also a need for studies to identify problems in achieving full design capacity.

Similar arguments were advanced against the supply under the new IDA commodity credit of power tillers, sprayers for pesticides and telecommunication and transport equipment. IDA considered that, once the immediate requirements for repair of war damage were met, any further addition to the capital stock in these fields should be judged by the standards and criteria applied to the finance of development projects through project assistance. The supply of additional sprayers for pesticides should be considered only after a cost–benefit study of the use of pesticides under the ruling system of distributing them without charge; free distribution, it was argued, encouraged inefficient and wasteful use of pesticide and, worse, a reckless use of them was potentially dangerous from the ecological point of view. In a similar vein the World Bank was willing to consider supplying inland water and telecommunications equipment under separate project assistance credits, which it encouraged Bangladesh to prepare and negotiate.

Bangladesh argued that the time taken and procedures involved in negotiating project assistance and securing disbursement of credit under such projects, were so time consuming as to impair Bangladesh's economic recovery. Delay could have costs more serious than a failure to optimise the use of aid in other respects.

The requirements of agriculture and industry represented two major categories and ceilings on expenditure in each category were imposed. In the first category, fertiliser and raw materials for leather manufacture were included; in the other, eleven industrial sub-categories were distinguished. Most of the credit was to meet industrial uses and two-thirds was for supplies for the jute, cotton textile, chemical and commercial vehicle industries. The allocations made under each category could be exceeded only with the Bank's previous permission.

The Bank expressed particular concern about two aspects of the utilisation of the commodity credit: the efficiency of the procedures of the import control system; and the system of marketing and distribution of items under the commodity credit within the country. In an effort to force changes it required the Government to improve its arrangements for allocating imports to priority uses, to ensure speedy and easy access to imports by actual users and to improve the access to finance of agencies, public and private, engaged in the importation and transportation of imports. A side letter, covering these matters, was exchanged when the credit agreement was signed. It obliged the Government to undertake a study of the import system and examine the institutional and administrative constraints affecting its import control system with a view to streamlining the arrangements. The terms of reference of the study were to be agreed between the Government and the Bank and the study report was to be followed by an exchange of views on the action that the Government might take to improve matters. The Government undertook to strengthen the administrative unit in the Planning Commission responsible for putting the credit into effect and monitoring its progress, the Government also agreed to inform IDA of the action that it proposed to take. Since IDA was particularly concerned about Bangaladesh's distribution plans for cotton and synthetic yarns, the Government was put under an obligation to provide such further information as IDA might require about distribution plans for items to be financed out of the credit and to hold itself ready for an exchange of views on these points.

The Government was in fact at least as anxious as was the Bank to improve importing arrangements and the distribution of goods. It was common knowledge that the distribution system was defective and aggravated shortages in the market which were felt most acutely in the countryside. By the middle of 1974, the

Government had strengthened the administrative unit in the Planning Commission which was responsible for IDA programme credits so as to expedite actions in all agencies concerned with the import process up to the time of shipment of goods. By the end of 1974, IDA and the Government had agreed on the terms and conditions of a study of the import system, which would be undertaken jointly by a foreign consultant or consultancy firm in co-operation with domestic counterparts, public or private. This study was to be financed by the technical assistance credit already provided by IDA. By the end of 1974, a third IDA import credit was extended.

As early as 1973, the World Bank felt that it should increasingly move from programme to project lending, since the charter and tradition of the Bank had a built-in bias in favour of project assistance. The Bank pointed out that Bangladesh's need for free foreign exchange for meeting balance of payment requirements would be provided in part by local cost financing included in project lending: some local cost financing could be justified in Bangladesh's case, the Bank argued, because of her low *per capita* income and consumption and scarcity of resources, domestic as well as foreign. Against this argument, Bangladesh pointed out that if IDA and other donors were to wait for project lending with local cost financing to provide the necessary foreign exchange, delays would be so long that in the intervening period, there would be acute distress and a major setback in development efforts.[2] Floods and other adversities of nature, as well as a serious deterioration in trade relations reflecting world inflation, made substantial increases in food and commodity aid necessary to prevent a fall in the level of essential imports. It was becoming increasingly obvious that without such imports industry would slow down and capacity and workers would remain idle, while essential consumer goods would become scarcer and prices rise. As it turned out, the Bank accepted that programme lending had to be a major feature of development aid to Bangladesh for quite some time.

Notes

1. *United Kingdom/Bangladesh Aid Grant*. Loan No. 2, 1974.
2. See chapter 3 for details of the slow rate of utilisation of project aid.

7 Food Aid

JACK PARKINSON

Before the partition of India the area now included in Bangladesh was largely self-sufficient in food, with the exception of major harvest failures such as that of 1943. Over the years the situation has changed drastically. In the 1950s the population growth progressively outran that of rice production and in most years half a million tons or more of grain had to be imported to ward off starvation. In the 1960s imports were often in the neighbourhood of one million tons and in the worst years of the 1970s over two million tons were needed. At times, a fifth or more of the population was dependent on imported supplies. The need for food exercised a stranglehold on the balance of payments; in the years 1973–6, 30 per cent to 40 per cent of imports consisted of food and during this period about one-third of total aid was in the form of food supplies.

Underlying these statistical trends lay the fundamental issue of whether it would be possible for Bangladesh to cross the threshold of simple survival to reach a stage of real development. Was it feasible to move from a state of high deficiency to one of near self sufficiency? Was there not a danger that massive food aid would in the end succeed only in prolonging the agony of individuals condemned to malnutrition, if not to premature death? These fears were shared by many; they would be assuaged only when efforts to increase the output of food and control the growth of the population showed evidence of success in bringing about a better balance.

In the meantime, Bangladesh's dependence on food aid involved the donors in discussions and negotiations on domestic policy matters, which had important consequences for production and income distribution, and for growth and equity. The ramifications of this were wide: from pricing policy under the rationing system and domestic procurement, to fiscal policy and wage policy; from these issues to measures to increase agricultural output and control the loss of food by smuggling; and inevitably to discussions of population policy. It put the aid-givers in the centre of discussions on all the crucial policy issues for the national survival and development of Bangladesh.

The major questions of food policy to which the donors addressed themselves were, first, the nature and coverage of the rationing system; second, the subsidy on rationed food; third, the case for domestic procurement of food to meet the needs of the rationing system; and ultimately, how, and how far they should exercise the influence over Bangladesh which the ability to prevent starvation conferred. We will now discuss these questions in turn, starting with issues raised by the administration of the food programmes.

The Rationing System

Food which was imported under aid or purchased by the Bangladesh Government, was distributed through the Government rationing system. This originally included three, and later on, four large urban centres, referred to as statutory rationing areas, in which every individual was entitled to a ration of grain, and bought in the open market only if this proved to be insufficient. The higher income groups in the urban areas did, in fact, supplement their ration by purchase in the open market. All Government employees were entitled to rations irrespective of residence.

Outside the statutory rationing areas, 'the modified rationing system' operated. In fact, the requirements of people living outside the towns were accorded secondary importance and they were considered only after the towns and Government employees were provided for. The population outside the statutory rationing areas was classified into four groups according to the amount of local taxes paid by different households which roughly reflects the income level.[1] Whatever supplies of grain were available were rationed according to a priority listing, starting with the poorest income classes. In addition, the Government distributed some free food to destitutes and beggars, particularly during natural calamities such as floods, cyclones and droughts when the poorest income groups were exposed to starvation.

About half a million tons of grain were needed annually to operate the statutory rationing system and a further one-third to one-half million tons were supplied to Government officers outside the statutory rationing areas and to flour mills which were entitled to a fixed quota. The allocation to the remaining beneficiaries of the public distribution system fluctuated, depending on availability on the one hand, and the extent of distress or shortage in the rural areas on the other.[2]

1974–5 was a year of acute distress, and in the third and fourth quarter of 1974 a famine of a magnitude unknown since 1943 ravaged the country. Since food aid did not come in time and in sufficient quantity, and since supplies to the statutory rationing areas and rations to Government employees were maintained on a priority basis, the brunt of the shortfall in supplies fell on those who came under the modified rationing system, with disastrous consequences for the poorest sections of the rural population and destitutes throughout the land. This was an inevitable result of a system under which a large fixed amount of subsidised food was distributed to Government employees and urban populations irrespective of their income levels, while the most vulnerable and poorest rural population had only residual claims on the grain available at the disposal of the Government.

It was not surprising that donors, as well as many nationals, questioned a rationing system which in times of extreme stringency would favour a privileged class of consumers and leave others vastly worse off to fend for themselves. Wartime systems of rationing were recalled, when the object had been to spread shortages evenly over the whole population, while producers themselves were obliged to place their output at the disposal of a general rationing system. Were there distinguishing features of the Bangladesh economy which made it right or necessary to give urban areas and all Government employees priority over the general rural populations? The urban areas undoubtedly did face acute supply shortages when domestic output was low and at these times there could be a large differential between rural and urban prices. When the output of food fell sharply, hoarding and speculation by intermediaries distorted the movement of supplies and forced prices to very high levels. Farmers, too, anticipating rising prices, were likely to hold on to stocks, thus interrupting the flow of food still further and driving prices to higher levels. Yet rationing itself could do little to even out the flow of supplies unless it was backed by stocks held by the Government and used to supplement supplies or by anticipatory adjustments in the flow of imports. Rationing is hardly relevant as a device to deal with speculation.

Food Subsidies

The price of foodgrains distributed under the rationing system was heavily subsidised. In 1973–4, a typical year, the cost of doing so amounted to Tk960 million, equivalent to about one-quarter of public sector development expenditure. The issue price was lower than either the world price or the free market domestic price.[3] Over the years, the prices of rationed rice and wheat were raised in an attempt to keep the total amount of subsidy from increasing when import prices rose.[4] But even in early 1975, when the worst effects of the 1974 famine had receded, the divergence between the price of rationed food and the cost of imports and free market domestic production was very considerable, as shown in Table 7.1.

TABLE 7.1 Prices of foodgrains, January 1975 (Taka per 2 lb.)

	Ration price	*Government cost*	*Free market price*
Rice	1.50	3.50	7.75
Wheat	1.25	2.00	6.00

The subsidy was very large and represented a heavy burden on the Government's budget. During 1973–4 the food subsidy was of an amount equivalent to the entire deficit in the non-development revenue budget. Even after the increase in the ration prices of wheat and rice in 1974, expenditure on food subsidies remained very high, falling to only Tk910 million in 1974–5, because of rising import prices. The subsidies were in effect financed by recourse to deficit financing with consequential inflationary effects. This was repeatedly pointed out by the

Finance and Planning Ministry officials and exports, as were the adverse effects of the urban oriented public distribution system on income distribution, which made no distinction between different income groups.

The net effect of the food subsidy on various groups of consumers is hard to assess: the result of a reduction or elimination of the subsidy might be good or ill, depending on the patterns and force of economic and political repercussions. The more affluent might have had to pay higher prices for part of their diet, but might also, to some extent, have benefited from a reduction in deficit financing and in the rate of inflation. On the face of it, the poor might have been expected to lose substantially. But even this is not certain: food subsidies, while ostensibly intended to ease the lot of the poor, do not always reach them in full because of deficiencies and diversions within the distribution system.

Donor agencies became explicitly involved in these policy issues when food aid was negotiated. They raised questions about the Government food distribution and pricing policy in the course of both bilateral aid negotiations and during the meetings of the Bangladesh aid consortium in 1974 and 1975. Donors voiced concern that only a minor proportion of food aid was distributed free to the poorest sections of the population and generally complained that food aid was not more fully and directly chanelled towards meeting the requirements of the poor.[5] They pointed out that when supplies were short, it was the poorest sections of the rural population that suffered most and were driven to make purchases at inflated and exorbitant prices; at such times they gained neither food nor subsidy. In Bangladesh's impoverished state, donors insisted, no valid case could be made for subsidising purchases of grain made by the relatively affluent. The United States apparently felt so strongly about the matter, including the budgetary effects of the subsidies, that, in late 1975, the USAID Mission decided to force a significant rise in ration prices by withholding a portion of food shipments in the period from November 1975 to March 1976.[6]

The basic problem of malnutrition and famine in Bangladesh is that landownership and tenure systems, prevailing technology and productivity, conditions of employment and income are such that the price at which it is economical to grow rice is so high that an adequate diet on a regular and sustained basis remains beyond the reach of large segments of the population. In the long run, the answer to this kind of problem might be found in the creation of employment opportunities by promoting labour intensive development in urban as well as rural areas. In the short run, income supplements or price subsidies, designed and operated with the explicit objective of offsetting the high price of food to those with insufficient incomes, may bring temporary relief. In fact PL 480 (the United States law under which food aid is provided) contains a clause that 'priority shall be given to countries which agree to use the proceeds from the sale of commodities . . . to increase the access of the poor in the recipient country to an adequate nutritious and stable food supply'[7]. Donors wanted 'their' food aid used in this manner and complained that the Government did not do so with the persistence and force which donors could consider commensurate with the needs of the difficult, at times desperate, food situation in the country. Interestingly the United States Government carefully avoided outright confrontation on this issue. It would have been open to it to have supplied aid under Title II of PL 480 instead of, as was mainly done, under Title I. Under Title II food distribution is normally contracted out to voluntary organisations which could have been required to distribute to the needy.[8]

Grain Procurement

The issue of the price at which foodgrain should be bought and sold was related to the issue of domestic procurement. A large part of the domestic output of foodgrain was consumed on the farms. The marketable surplus of home produced food, constituting up to one-fifth of total output, was provided mainly by the 2 million or so larger farm units; farmers with less than three acres contributed little. The *per capita* consumption of cereals of the surplus farmers was higher than the national average and may have amounted to about 17–18 ounces against a fluctuating national average of about 15 ounces per adult per day, and much lower figures for those in extreme poverty. Making allowance for rice production consumed on the farm and used to compensate farm labourers for work performed, the total amount of food distributed through the market and the rationing system might amount to perhaps 4 million tons of which about half might be from home sources. A small proportional variation in overall domestic output leads to a considerably larger proportional change in the marketable surplus. Even a moderate shortfall in domestic production thus has the effect of increasing the need for imports very sharply. If, in such circumstances, imports are not forthcoming in time and in adequate amounts, the poorest sections of the population and those who depend on the modified rationing system are exposed to disastrous deprivation and famine. Some foodgrain was procured by the Government in the domestic market before independence, both on a voluntary and a compulsory basis, but the amounts were not very substantial; it exceeded 100,000 tons only in three years and was often substantially less than this figure. The highest amount procured was about 200,000 tons in 1959, when there was a very good harvest, and it was achieved under the full force of the martial law administration which had just been introduced.[9] Although the procurement in 1959 was largely voluntary, it was accompanied by 'cordoning' off surplus areas, thus preventing movement of foodgrain between different regions of the country.

In the post independence period, the first systematic attempt at procurement was made in 1973–4. It was designed to be voluntary except in the areas bordering India. Within a ten mile radius of the border all farmers were required to surrender a stipulated share of their surplus stocks.[10] The rice mills in the border areas were required to surrender their entire output to the Government. Otherwise, there was no restriction on the movement of foodgrain from surplus to deficit areas. The prices fixed by the Government in some areas were less than the ruling market price; procurement prices followed, rather than led the free market prices. The total amount procured was barely 70,000 tons and negligible in relation to the 1.7 million tons distributed under the rationing system during the year.

During 1974–5 the Government introduced compulsory procurement and prohibited movement of foodgrain from surplus areas, which it designated. The rice mills in the border areas were again required to surrender their entire output to the Government, and the farmers in the border areas had to surrender a larger proportion of their surplus than those in the hinterland. The amount procured was 130,000 tons, appreciably more than in the previous year, but still very small in relation to the quantity needed for the rationing system. Because of the greater scarcity in

1974–5, imports, as well as the amounts procured domestically, were much larger in that year than in 1973–4.

Although compulsory procurement in 1974–5, coupled with the ban on movement of foodgrain from the surplus districts, was effective in increasing purchases, it was feared that it would seriously discourage farmers from increasing their output. Much depended on the price offered. Even in 1973–4, when procurement was voluntary and when the price offered by the Government corresponded fairly closely to the ruling market price, farmers were reluctant to sell to Government purchasing agents because of formalities involved in conducting transactions with Government agencies; adjustments made for quality and incidence of wet paddy, and payment by cheque or through banks. There was a case for the Government paying a slightly higher price than private traders in order to attract substantial purchases. In 1974–5 the disincentive effects were aggravated by 'cordoning' off surplus areas and the compulsory nature of procurement.

In fixing appropriate procurement prices, the Government faced a dilemma. On the one hand, low prices would discourage production and would provide strong incentives for violation of the laws regarding the movement of foodgrain as well as for smuggling across the border to India. (Such smuggling took place at the highly depreciated black market rate of exchange of the Bangladesh Taka for the Indian Rupee, and so was highly profitable.) On the other hand, a high price would increase the amount of subsidy involved if the price of rationed food was not increased. As the international price of foodgrain (at the offical rate of exchange) was very much lower than the domestic free market price, substitution of domestically procured food for imported foodgrain in the rationing system, even without putting up the price to farmers, substantially increased the amount of subsidy involved. If domestically procured food were substituted for imported food in the rationing system, either the selling price of rationed food or the subsidy would have to be increased.[11]

The system of compulsory procurement proved difficult to operate. The larger the farmer, the more likely it was that he would evade the controls and engage in smuggling and other sales outside the Government's procurement system. For the small farmer it was hard to assess the surplus, and decide how much should be appropriated, and generally to distribute the burden equitably. If purchases were to be appreciable, then a very large number of farmers had to be approached. The smaller the farmer, the more likely it was that any surplus would be consumed rather than marketed willingly, and greater pressure was consequently necessary to secure supplies. The offer of a remunerative price was particularly important in the case of small farmers.

A variety of approaches for assessing the surplus stock available for procurement have been tried. In some years, surplus foodgrain was calculated after taking into account farmers' consumption requirements and expenses to be met in kind, and procurement was confined to farmers above a certain minimum size; in most cases, the percentage of surplus procured was graduated according to the size of the farms. In other years, a levy was imposed on all farmers above a certain size, and was graduated according to the size of the farms; this was administratively simple and avoided the problem of estimating the surplus of output over requirements. Thus, during 1974–5, there was no exemption limit and all farmers were subject to procurement according to a prescribed scale; output was estimated by multiplying the area under different types of rice crop by the estimated average yield per acre for each crop. The estimate of the surplus was to be made by committees consisting of officers, representatives of political parties and selected members of the local elite. The ostensible purpose of this method was to mobilise popular support, ensure a more accurate assessment of the surplus available, and facilitate its procurement. Obviously, the system could be frustrated in various ways; the members of the committee might be influenced by those affected to reduce the quantities required from them; and since paddy produced in border areas was subject to a higher rate of levy it might be transported to the hinterland (or even smuggled to India) as a means of evasion.

Experience with procurement operations in Bangladesh has shown that farmers are more willing to co-operate if the paddy procured is kept in their own locality rather than shifted to other areas. This may reflect a fear that in the event of a future shortage caused by natural calamity or otherwise, supplies would not be made available to them in time. Clearly it is not always possible to store foodgrain where they are produced, but a policy of distributing stocks widely and retaining some reserves in the surplus areas, in some instances, has proved conducive to acceptance by the farmer of Government procurement.

An alternative to direct procurement considered by the Government was to levy taxes payable in kind in the form of foodgrain, which could be stored in the village godowns. Stocks collected in this way would have been available for distribution to landless labourers and deficit farmers in the villages or unions from which the foodgrain came, as well as to deficit areas outside. Such a tax, if politically practicable, could reasonably have been imposed on those who benefited from the supply of fertiliser, pesticides, credit and irrigation water at subsidised prices. A further possibility considered was to provide modern inputs in kind to the farmers and to obtain repayment in foodgrain at harvesting time, using the village co-operatives to organise the operation.

The experience of food procurement in the early years of Bangladesh in different circumstances and by different methods was closely examined by Government planners and experts. The depth and coverage of their analysis went far beyond the simple suggestion by aid-givers that foodgrain should be procured on a voluntary basis at market prices from surplus farmers in order to meet the requirements of urban dwellers at non-subsidised prices. It was not shortage of ideas or insight that held back change but political factors.

Donor Influence on Food Policy

Donors disapproved of the policy of subsidising food and were prepared to countenance it only if it were directed towards the poorest income groups: even then they thought it should be eliminated gradually. They strongly favoured domestic procurement at prices which would give an incentive to farmers to increase production and marketing. As time went on the donors became increasingly concerned that food aid was being used to feed a high income urban population, and that the rationing system for the whole urban population depended exclusively on imports. They suspected that even if the domestic supply of food was increased, the need for imports would not decline because much of the increase would be consumed by the farmers themselves and very little of any surplus produced would in fact be channelled to the urban population, thus reducing the need for imported food. Donors' views on food policy in Bangladesh as they had developed by 1975 are most clearly expressed in summary form in a published report by the Canadian International Development Agency:[12]

> 'The bulk of the foodgrains imports are sold at subsidized prices to ration card holders who for the most part belong to the Bangladesh urban middle class. Locally produced foodgrains should increasingly meet the group's needs and food aid should be directed towards the poorest elements of society. Better statistics are needed on food production, distribution and requirements to support food aid requirements. More attention should be given, first, to shortfall in food production, and second, to improving the present rationing system.
>
> While there is only limited free distribution of food, the 'work for food' programme, sponsored by the Government of Bangladesh, by international organisations and by non-governmental agencies, provides significant sectors of the population with a minimum quantity of food. The supply of food by the Government of Bangladesh for the operation of these programmes is, however, far short of the people's need and the capacity of such programme.
>
> Despite some recent improvements, the rural landless – most of them without work – get an extremely meagre share of rationed food, while the system takes care first of the urban areas, and within rural areas, gives priority to the army, teachers and public servants.
>
> The Government has also adopted a policy to procure locally grown rice to ensure a fair distribution of the national production. The results, up to now, are limited but may be regarded as a significant start.
>
> Concern has been expressed on the part of the Government of Canada to the Government of Bangladesh as to the fair distribution of Canadian and other international food aid and nationally produced rice, and assurance has been received that these objections are pursued actively, with already visible results.'

On the future role of Canadian food aid, the report recommended continued food aid to Bangladesh and stated that:

'Canada should continue to express to the Government of Bangladesh the concern of Canadians about leakages and the lack of equitable distribution of food and locally grown rice. It should support efforts of the government of Bangladesh to strengthen its controls over procurement and supply, to improve the distribution system, and to place more emphasis on directing rationed food to the poorest segments of society, particularly in the rural areas.'

The report was clear about the ends that it sought to achieve but it had little to say about all the practical issues that would have to be solved if an effective procurement system were to be successfully operated.

Domestic procurement of foodgrain was never specified as a formal condition of providing food aid in legal documents; but it was much discussed and played a critical role in all negotiations on the supply of food; in effect, it became a condition precedent for any increase in food aid allocations made by major donors. At best, procurement could go only part of the way to easing the food shortage. It would not eliminate the need for imports; nor could it reduce fluctuations in yields which were magnified by speculative influences; only building up reserve stocks could frustrate speculation and hoarding on the part of private traders. Nevertheless donors began to see aid and procurement as having two different functions. They suggested that food aid should be directed towards meeting the needs of the poor sectors of the population, whereas domestically procured food should meet the requirements of the high income, urban dwellers. An extension of the argument might have been that reduction in food aid would compel the Government to resort to domestic procurement to meet the demands of the rationing system.

It may be instructive to bring out some orders of magnitude involved. If all imported foodgrain, say 2 million tons, had been used for subsidised rationing for the poor, nearly the whole lowest fifth of the population would have been adequately supplied without exceeding the amount of budgetary outlay imposed under the actual operation of the urban biased public distribution system. If it had been intended to undertake non-inflationary financing of the cost of subsidy on the food distributed to the poor, it would have been necessary to have found additional sources of Government revenue, perhaps by taxing farm income above a certain level and profits derived from both internal trade and imports. It must be recognised, however, that in calculations of this sort subsidies for the poor imply commensurate reduction in consumption of non-food items by the poor themselves or in overall consumption by the better off.

The Government would probably have responded quite quickly to the pressures of donors to change its food policies if the issues had been purely economic. However, even seven years after independence and after dramatic changes in Government structure and personalities, a basic change in food policy in Bangladesh has yet to be made. The overriding reason for this is quite simply that the policy of providing subsidised food to all Government employees (including those in the armed forces) and to the whole urban population, irrespective of income, reflects the realities of politics and power in the country. The urban middle class, the industrial workers, the officers and men in the army and administration constitute vocal, volatile, and organised groups which would create disorder, incite dissatisfaction and threaten the political *status quo* if estranged. These governing elements of the population, minuscule in number but overwhelmingly powerful, have grown accustomed to their privileged position, including the supply of cheap rations of food. By contrast, the rural poor remain unorganised and as a silent majority in the political structure constitute no immediate threat. The Government's policy is not designed to help the poor at the cost of eroding the positions of power and privilege of the few; it is designed to meet the Government's strongly felt need to secure its political position. This was the situation in the early years of Bangladesh, it could hardly have been otherwise. It remains the situation under the successive Governments in the post Mujib era.

The leadership and power structure of Bangladesh is, of course, not monolithic or without diversity of interests and views. Many policy makers within Government shared the criticisms of the food pricing, procurement and distribution policies as voiced by donors.

Reforms of the rationing system were seen to be needed. The great divergence between free market and ration prices, gave the incentive of personal gain for any administrators willing to provide extra ration cards in return for illegal income, or to withhold ration cards in the absence of a bribe. The dealers or intermediaries in the distribution of rationed food had an incentive to sell it on the black market at high prices, or to sell additional amounts to selected customers while providing inadequate supplies to others, on grounds of 'inadequate deliveries' by the central agency, which could not be checked and supervised. The high price in the free market for foodgrain also provided an incentive for forging and stealing ration cards. The rural population was particularly prone to these abuses because it was difficult to give the far flung modified rationing scheme adequate surveillance.

In the interest of procuring food for the urban areas much can be said for taxing surplus farmers. There was and remains, however, considerable reluctance to increase the weight of taxation, even to the limited extent of eliminating subsidies. The composition of the public leadership in the country and the Government in the early years was such as to give power to large farmers, who naturally sought to exercise their influence so as to remain outside the net of taxes. Similarly, there was great reluctance to step up the procurement of grain significantly in the face of the opposition that such programmes aroused.

At the level of administration, there were doubts in the minds of many as to how fast and how efficiently the Government could move, if indeed it so decided, in the direction of a major reform of the food system. The administrative capacity of the Government was already strained and was not up to the added responsibility that new policies would impose. The need for a widely dispersed system of godowns and warehouses in the country as well as for efficient intermediaries to do the purchasing on behalf of the Government was greater than could readily be met. The success of local organisations and local initiative, with broad based participation of the farmers, would be essential for ensuring roughly equitable sharing of the burden of procurement among the farmers with minimum abuses and disincentive effects on the production of foodgrain. If supplies were to be brought on to the market by the imposition of taxes and revision of pricing policies for agricultural inputs and outputs, it would at best take time to gain the acceptance of such impositions. Moreover, it had been one of the political planks of the Awami League that land tax on all but the largest holdings should be abolished and it would be hard to find political support for a reversal of this position.

In their dealings with Government on issues of general food policy in Bangladesh the donors on balance probably had a helpful, yet marginal influence. They did represent a force for an expanded 'food for work' programme to cater for the needs of weaker sections of the rural population. They did contribute to the realisation that the best way to help the rural poor was through rural development projects and programmes which could create employment and provide income to buy food and other basic necessities. They probably on balance did strengthen the hands of their allies in these matters within the Planning Commission and the Finance Ministry in attempts to secure some reform, by pointing out the ineffiencies and abuses of the prevailing system of public distribution and pricing of foodgrain. They did expose the inequities of the public distribution system with its urban bias and relative neglect of the poor, rural population. They did contribute to a more explicit recognition of the economic cost of political constraints and compulsions. However, they did not – contrary to what they appeared to be seeking – change or influence the underlying realities of political life in the country. In the general area of food policy in Bangladesh the donors represented a force for marginal reform in details; their influence on the balance of political and social structures was at best negligible, at times an irritant which could be shrugged off.

Politics and Diplomacy of Food Aid

Imports of foodgrain are by far the major source of supplies for the public food rationing system, which covers about 15 per cent of total consumption in the country and at times as much as 90 per cent of consumption in the towns. Timely and adequate flows of grain imports are therefore essential for the smooth operation of the rationing system. Given the large annual and seasonal variations in domestic output, and in view of the low level of stocks of foodgrain held in the early years of Bangladesh, the flow of imports in fact could not be adjusted sufficiently quickly enough always to ensure that adequate supplies were available. This would have required a more reliable early warning system on crop prospects within the country, and guarantees of priority shipment under aid or through commercial contracts from the major world suppliers, notably from the USA. In actual fact these requirements could not be met. As a result, the rations sometimes had to be cut when they were most needed, with calamitous consequences in some instances. Also, the variable but heavy reliance on food imports and food aid placed Bangladesh in a position of recurring dependence for survival on major foreign countries, which could and did exercise their 'food power'. During the early years of Bangladesh the ramifications of its food dependence were evidenced in many ways, sometimes dramatically.

In the summer of 1973 there was a serious shortage of food supplies for the rationing system, in part due to an unanticipated delay in the commitment and shipment of grain from the USA. The only way the requirements could be met in time was by diverting supplies of food already at sea, intended for other destinations, to Bangladesh. In principle, US food aid could be diverted to Bangladesh on condition that it would be replenished by Bangladesh from its own shipments later on. There was also the possibility that an importing country which had purchased grain commercially could divert supplies to Bangladesh, which could be made good later out of aid shipments. At the time, the USSR had purchased large quantities of foodgrain, from the USA as well as other countries, and was in a position to divert shipment of such food at short notice to Bangladesh. Delivery was completed between July and October 1973. Bangladesh was planning to repay the Russian wheat loan out of shipments of PL 480 wheat which Bangladesh was due to receive from the USA towards the end of 1973, and it made an early request to the United States to agree to this arrangement. It appears that the USA was not agreeable to this given the constraints at the time on the availabilities of US supplied grain, as well as the statutory impediments that had to be taken into account. In the event, Bangladesh could not procure sufficient supplies to meet domestic requirements and also to repay the borrowed wheat; she was, therefore, driven to reach a financial arrangement for repayment.

Bangladesh had to learn to adjust to the fact that food aid from the US was subject to domestic pressure groups and vested interests there. One expression of this was the changing proportions of rice and wheat that were made available. Beyond a certain point, and in spite of its traditional preference for rice, Bangladesh preferred to purchase wheat rather than rice, because the latter was much more expensive.[13] In the course of negotiation on food aid towards the end of 1974, when Bangladesh's import needs were high and urgent, it appeared that an increasing quantity of wheat could be obtained only in combination with an increasing quantity of rice. The pressure to export rice from the USA seemed to be due to the farmers' lobby reacting to a bumper crop of rice in 1974.[14] With a given money value of food assistance, an increased proportion of rice would have the effect of reducing the quantum of food available to Bangladesh. However, Bangladesh was assured that the rise in the proportion of rice would not reduce the amount of wheat below what otherwise would have been available to Bangladesh.

When food aid was supplied by the USA under PL 480, the recipient country was subjected to conditions restricting its freedom of action in external trade, specifically trade with a list of countries stipulated by policy makers in the USA. A most serious food shortage, culminating in the period August to October, was threatening Bangladesh in 1974, and an early renewal of the agreement with the USA for the supply of foodgrain was seen at the beginning of the summer to be of critical importance in order to ensure increased and immediate shipment. The course of events is far from clear and not fully documented publicly, but the following description captures the essentials.

In June 1974 it was brought to the notice of the Bangladesh Government that the PL 480 Act, as amended in 1966, disqualified any country which exported (sold or furnished commodities) to Cuba or North Vietnam, or allowed vessels under its registry to call at the ports of these countries, from receiving assistance under the act.[15] The US law permitted only limited exceptions to its stipulated provisions, but a presidential waiver might be made in respect of sales of non-strategic agricultural commodities and non-strategic raw materials for agriculture or medical supplies, provided also that the waiver was in the national interest of the USA.

Early in 1974, however, the Government of Bangladesh, unaware of this provision of the PL 480 Act, had contracted to sell 4 million jute bags to Cuba. Before signing the PL 480 agreement therefore, the Government of the USA needed an assurance from the Bangladesh Government that it did not intend to permit Government agencies or Government corporations to export to Cuba or to permit vessels under Bangladesh registration to call at Cuban ports. Effectively any trade of Bangladesh with Cuba was banned so long as Bangladesh needed to be a recipient of food aid under PL 480. Moreover in the critical months of 1974, the requirements of PL 480 could be interpreted to imply that Bangladesh could be said not to be selling jute goods to Cuba, only after the last shipment had left Bangladesh ports. The contract with Cuba had been concluded early in 1974, but due to lack of shipping space, despatch was delayed and it was October before the last shipment took place. A shipment of 73,000 tons of wheat was reported in the *Washington Post* of 20 September, 1974 as having arrived in Bangladesh from the USA in July. No further shipments are mentioned and there seems to have been a total gap in deliveries between then and December 1974. No attempt also seems to have been made to anticipate the signing of a new agreement and to despatch food in the expectation that the Cuban incident would be resolved. It was not until 30 September that the *Washington Post* was able to indicate the likelihood that a new contract would be signed within a few days. In the intervening months, in August and September, the worst famine in Bangladesh in twenty-five years occurred; thousands of people died of starvation.[16]

The embargo on supplies under PL 480 to countries trading with Cuba also affected supplies of edible oil to Bangladesh under the PL 480 agreement signed in 1973. By the time the Cuba episode was over, the US had placed an embargo on all exports of edible oil because of domestic scarcity and high prices, with the result that the delayed shipment of edible oil never took place and Bangladesh went short. While the break in food shipments from the United States appears to have been largely the result of decisions taken in relation to Cuba, the official US Aid position was that stocks in Bangladesh had been adequate to prevent mass starvation and hunger and that it had been decided to give priority to other areas of the world. It is also reported that 'security assistance' had been given priority in Kissinger's instructions to Government policy makers. In this case the Cuban incident might have been no more than a pretext to take Bangladesh off the list of food and recipients. It may be recalled that Egypt's trade with Cuba was said not to be in contention; cotton shipments from that country to Cuba appeared to be excludable under the terms of the 1967 law although no such exclusion appeared to be possible for gunny sacks made in Bangladesh. For American subsidiaries of Ford, General Motors and Chrysler in Argentina there was no difficulty in obtaining export licences.[17]

The hard lesson of this experience was that food supplies even from friendly foreign countries cannot be relied upon and that even an inadvertent breaking of rules set by the supplying country can lead to extreme deprivation. It is not a trivial matter for a poor country with a tenuous food balance to be caught up in the political concerns of other countries.

Notes

1. Group A consisted of the poorest classes paying no union taxes, and having a monthly income of not more than Tk100. This group included all the landless and the vast majority of deficit farmers. Group B were those who paid union tax of Tk3 and had a monthly income of not more than Tk200. Group C were those who paid a tax of Tk5 and had a monthly income of not more than Tk300. Group D included all other citizens.
2. The amount distributed in 1972–3 exceeded 2.5 million tons. With nearly 1 million tons needed for priority distribution to the statutory rationing areas, to Government officers and the flour mills, about 1.5 million tons were available for distribution outside the major towns under the modified rationing system. In the following year, 1973–4, the amount available for distribution under the modified rationing system dropped by 50 per cent. Cf. *Statistical Pocket Book of Bangladesh 1978*, Bangladesh Bureau of Statistics, Dacca, 1978, p. 379.
3. At the official exchange rate the domestic market price was considerably higher than the world market price. This comparison may be spurious, however, since the Taka was overvalued, at least up to mid-1975.
4. The price ratio between rice and wheat under the rationing system, which in 1973–4 was 4 to 3 was reduced in 1974–5 to 6 to 5 in recognition of the fact that the consumers in Bangladesh had become accustomed to eating wheat, and that the strong preference for rice as against wheat had diminished.
5. At one point, some donors, who provided food in the form of outright grants, argued that the Bangladesh Government also should distribute all this food free.
6. See Donald F. McHenry and Kai Bird, 'Food for Aid and Diplomacy', *Foreign Policy*, Summer 1977, p. 84.
7. Ibid., p. 83.
8. Ibid., p. 76.
9. It is interesting that with the very good harvest of 1977–8 and suitable pricing policies, it proved possible to procure about 0.5 million tons of foodgrain.
10. Surplus stocks were estimated at that time as the difference between production and requirements for consumption and seed, reckoned as 0.66 maund (80 lb.) of paddy per family member per month up to the next

harvesting season, plus one maund of paddy per acre of land to use as seed, plus 20 maunds for miscellaneous requirements.

11. Also, of course, to the extent domestically procured food was substituted for food imported under aid, no counterpart funds were generated and the overall budgetary position deteriorated correspondingly.
12. *Report to the Secretary of State for External Affairs on the Mission to Bangladesh, March 19–21 1975*, by Paul Gérin-Lajoie, President, Canadian International Development Agency.
13. In fact, wheat was fairly readily consumed as a substitute for rice in Bangladesh at the prices fixed for sale of imported grain, provided also a certain minimum quantity of rice was obtained from abroad.
14. The same seems to have been true when the USA had a surplus of rice in 1976 at a time when Bangladesh did not have enough storage room even for domestically produced rice and feared that importation might reduce local prices and so production. See Francis Moore Lappé and Joseph Collins with Cary Fowler, *Food First*, Houghton Mifflin, Boston, 1977, p. 341.
15. McHenry and Bird, op. cit., p. 82, write that when the United States' Ambassador informed the Planning Commission of the position, the reaction was one of shocked surprise that the United States should insist that a destitute Bangladesh should restrict its exports. They comment as following: 'The United States' Government employed its food aid leverage in Bangladesh for the most trifling of political purposes.'
16. See also the account by Emma Rothschild, 'Food Politics', in *Foreign Affairs*, Vol. 54 (1976), No. 2, page 296:

> 'Early in 1974, the Bangladesh Government contracted to buy grain to meet its import needs from Canada, Australia and the United States. These purchases, at current high market prices, were to be financed with short-term commercial credit. In the summer of 1974 Bangladesh. . . . was unable to obtain the credit. Two large sales by American grains companies for delivery in the Autumn were therefore cancelled . . . Meanwhile U.S. agreements to supply food as aid under the PL 480 program were also delayed, mainly because officials were negotiating in secret as to whether Bangladesh was disqualified from receiving aid because it had sold jute to Cuba earlier in the year. [A Treasury official suggested afterwards that 'at least at the Treasury', officials also considered triage-like ideas as to where the prevention of famine would be most useful.] By the time the American food arrived in Bangladesh, in December 1974, the Autumn famine was over.'

17. See the *Washington Post*, 30 September, 1974: 'Dacca Aid tied to Cuban Ban'.

Part Three:

Donor Co-ordination and Collective Leverage

8 The Bangladesh Aid Group

JUST FAALAND

The 1973 Conference

While in its early years Bangladesh found it difficult to accept the idea of an aid donors' consortium as a ready solution to the problems of aid co-ordination, it was not rejected altogether, and was kept under review.[1] The issue was discussed with many of the potential members of a consortium in the hope that it might be possible to develop some form of regular meetings, that would be acceptable both to Bangladesh and to donor participants. As seen from Bangladesh, however, it became apparent that donors found it difficult to visualise other ways of organising consortia meetings than those they were already accustomed to, and particularly that they had closed their minds to the possibility that the lead in the organisation of consortium meetings might be taken by the recipient country. It appeared possible, however, that donors might be ready to accept an alternative venue for the consortium meeting, other than Washington or Paris. This led to the suggestion that it might be instructive and rewarding for Bangladesh to organise a meeting in Dacca of donor countries and agencies.

As pressures from donors for the establishment of a consortium built up in 1972 the Government took the initiative in sounding out donors on their willingness to meet in Dacca under the chairmanship of Bangladesh. A form of meeting bearing similarity to consortia meetings was proposed and the basic subject matter for discussion was to be much the same; it was specifically proposed that the meeting would consider Bangladesh development problems and prospects and the foreign assistance required for the ensuing year, as might have been done in a consortium meeting. The idea was opposed by the World Bank and a few major donors. They took the view that a meeting should not be chaired by Bangladesh as a recipient country or held in its capital, Dacca. It was better for the organisation and management of the consortium to be left to an institution like the World Bank, which, it was argued, because it had both donors and recipients as members, could be impartial. It was difficult for Bangladesh to accept this view: the Bank was dominated in terms of ownership, control and management by the donor countries; it was also an interested party, like any donor country, because it had large aid programmes in Bangladesh. More understandable was the fear that holding a meeting in Dacca might set a precedent, which could be followed by other recipient countries. When matters of principle against a meeting in Dacca were refuted, logistics were introduced: it would be difficult to organise secretarial assistance, documentation, transport and other facilities in Dacca, and it might not be possible to attract appropriately high ranking delegations. Another argument against such a meeting was that it would be more subject to leakage to the local press and that this would inhibit free and frank discussion as well as expose the Bangladesh Government to political attack and the accusation of bowing to pressures from donors. This argument carried some weight at one point during the deliberations because it seemed that elections might possibly follow the meeting of donors in an emotionally charged atmosphere.

Some of the objections to a meeting of donors in Dacca were expressed by large donors; most of them were aired by the World Bank, which took it upon itself to represent the donors and discuss their reactions with the Bangladesh Government. The latter made its own enquiries and gained the impression that most donors did not see any difficulty to meeting in Dacca and did not think that the composition of the delegations would suffer because of the venue. Donor country representatives may have felt it incumbent to reply in this way to an embarrasing question; nevertheless the Bangladesh Government was left with the impression that the main obstacle to holding a meeting in Bangladesh was the attitude of the Bank, whose primary objection appeared to be the fear that it would set a pattern for future meetings. The Bangladesh Government sought to allay this fear by making it clear that options for the future would remain open. In the end, when agreement to holding a meeting in Dacca at the end of March 1973 was finally reached, the Bank as well as the IMF offered to give logistic support and to share the preparation of documents for the meeting with the Bangladesh Government, as was customary for regular consortia meetings. The Bank circulated a report on the Bangladesh economy prepared in the latter part of 1972, and the Bangladesh Government presented an analysis of foreign assistance requirements and of the economic situation and the way in which it was expected to develop. The Five Year Plan was not ready at the time but its outlines were disclosed and circulated to the delegations, as was a detailed paper on requirements of technical assistance.

Nineteen countries and international agencies were invited to what was termed the International Conference on the Development of Bangladesh. In its letter of invitation, the Government of Bangladesh emphasised that the meeting would enable the donors to see the country for themselves, so gaining direct contact and first hand acquaintance with its economy, and to talk to those responsible for policy making and development administration and for the implementation of development projects. The Government expressed the hope that donors would be able to quantify aid commitments to Bangladesh for the year 1973–4. It declared its readiness to discuss any questions about policies, strategies and programmes with participating countries. Holding the meeting in Dacca would allow the Planning Commission, which was in charge of aid negotiations, including matters relating to aid co-ordination, to seek authoritative political guidance when necessary.

In the meeting each delegate was invited to make a statement, raising points he considered important or of particular concern. The proceedings were formal and there was no open discussion of the initial statements. When they had all made their set speeches, the Bangladesh Delegation selected those points to which it wanted to respond and made a statement on issues it considered important. The range of issues covered was very large and two days proved to be too short a period to have a full discussion of the whole field. Nevertheless the discussion succeeded in highlighting those questions which were uppermost in the minds of the donors, which could then be discussed subsequently.

The outline of the Five-Year Plan that had been circulated to delegations gave rise to a general discussion. There was fairly general agreement with its broad priorities. The emphasis on agriculture and rural development and employment and the awareness of the Government about the seriousness of the problem of the growth of population in Bangladesh was favourably received. Doubts were expressed about the size of the planned development programme, which was felt to be too big and beyond Bangladesh's resources. There was discussion of the appropriate role for the public sector in development, which some countries believed to be overemphasised and liable totally to displace private investment. Several delegations expressed the view that greater weight needed to be placed on the utilisation of capacity in the industrial sector, combined with a better integration of large- and small-scale industry.

A great deal of comment was made on the estimate of the overall food shortage, its relation to import requirements and the need to increase agricultural output. What was the optimum cropping pattern in agriculture? Was the emphasis on rice production at the expense of jute and crops such as wheat or vegetables, which contributed to a balanced and nutritionally adequate diet, well placed? What attempts were being made to encourage production of wheat? What were the essential components of the rice production programme? Since jute was a key element in the balance of payments, questions were put about the pricing policy being followed in order to make it competitive with synthetics. This led to questions about the prospects of non-jute exports, such as fish and leather.

As might be expected, concern was expressed about domestic inflation and about credit and exchange rate policies, where the IMF is regarded as the authority. Project preparation was frequently referred to as being deficient. Questions and comments were directed to the role that could and should be played by technical assistance and expatriate experts in planning and executing development projects.

In reply the Bangladesh Delegation described how the size of the plan was justified. Government policy towards the private sector was explained, as was the importance of maintaining small-scale and cottage industries. The assistance that the private sector would need and could expect from the Government was described, as well as the reasons why it was thought desirable to have a large public sector. The components of the agricultural programme and the need for irrigation, credit and fertilisers were detailed, the desirability of research on jute cultivation was pointed out, and experiments to increase wheat production explained. Most of these explanations were in the nature of a repetition of what was already included in the written documentation.

More general discussions related to the state of project preparation in different sectors of the economy. The identification of worthwhile projects in the field of water and agriculture was at a fairly advanced stage, because of the work undertaken in this field before liberation by international agencies, particularly the World Bank, and subsequently by the Government of Bangladesh. A document containing a list of high priority projects in these areas with a short explanatory note indicating the need for further studies was circulated among the participants of the meeting.

There was only a limited opportunity to discuss the participation of donor countries individually and together in the broad context of the aid programmes, although important issues were raised. One issue raised was that while some countries provided soft loans with a major grant element, there were others who charged much harder terms and thus were getting repaid at the expense of the soft lenders. Food exporters were also concerned that they should not be asked to provide a disproportionate share of food aid. Bangladesh sought to impress on the meeting that the country needed outright grants and loans on the softest of terms; it also emphasised the need for programme aid and for local cost financing. Support in principle for this position was expressed by some participants. A few countries, in particular the Scandinavian countries, were in favour of introducing a greater degree of certainty or continuity in aid programming so that Bangladesh could plan on the basis of indicative figures of aid available in future years. They indicated tentative figures of aid commitment for the next three or four years. By contrast, far from supplying indicative figures for several years, some countries were unable to provide an estimate even for one year. This reflected concentration on a project by project approach by which the amount of development assistance actually received would depend on the cost of the projects agreed between the two countries.

Scandinavian country representatives stressed the need for providing assistance to Bangladesh within the context of the socio-political goals decided by the Government; Bangladesh had proclaimed its adherence to a socialist economic system within a democratic framework and her preference should be accepted by the donors. These countries argued that maximum benefit from assistance would be obtained only if it were consistent with socio-political goals. They percipiently warned against too great a dependence by Bangladesh on foreign aid, indicating that donors could be a fairly dangerous crowd who should be feared despite the gifts they might bring or the promises they might convey. Too much foreign assistance could have a tendency to distort priorities set by Bangladesh.

In all these respects the meeting took the normal path of polite exchanges in a diplomatic context following an agreed agenda. There was one issue which explicitly had been excluded from the agenda of the meeting but which nearly every delegate mentioned on the first day: the problem of the outstanding debt liability of Pakistan and the share thereof which might be allocated to Bangladesh. This issue was to bedevil relationships between Bangladesh and the international donor community from the foundation of Bangladesh until it was finally resolved in the summer of 1974. Nothing that happened in the field of aid negotiations can be understood if this point is not fully grasped. We return to this issue in Chapter 9 and discuss it at length as an exercise in leverage designed to force Bangladesh's acceptance of a share of the debt liability of Pakistan under the threat of withdrawal of development assistance. It has to be mentioned here, for the fact that it was raised at the 1973 meeting in the way described, was to have the effect of seriously damaging relations between Bangladesh and Western aid donors.

The crucial issue was whether, when and to what extent Bangladesh would accept a share of Pakistan's debt liability. Absence of the issue from the agenda made no difference to the delegations; it was raised nonetheless in a pre-determined and concerted move to impress upon the Bangladesh Government the serious view donors took of what they considered its unwillingness to come to terms. Although the reasons for this had been fully explained in bilateral discussions between individual donors and Bangladesh, they insisted on an answer satisfactory to them before they would pledge further development support. Bangladesh made it clear that it would rather go without pledges of assistance, than accept conditional ones. Nevertheless, practically all delegations persisted in announcing such conditional pledges.

This first major exposure of Bangladesh to a meeting of donors as a group left its mark on subsequent developments towards an organised aid group for Bangladesh. It seemed to Bangladesh to be a moot point as to whether more aid, on better terms and in more convenient forms, would be forthcoming if a traditional type consortium were set up than if it were decided to continue to do without it. But even assuming that there were to be some such advantage in doing so, doubts remained about the desirability of having the meetings chaired by the World Bank and about the advantages of holding such meetings away from Dacca. The incident of co-ordinated donor pressures in respect of Pakistan's debt liabilities confirmed the worst fears of the Government: a consortium of donors was indeed liable to be used to exercise aid leverage on the recipient country. The role of the World Bank as a determined organiser of creditors, not primarily an international instrument of mediation, was seen as being exposed beyond doubt. Those donor delegates who had urged the formation of a regular consortium for aid to Bangladesh at an early date had clearly failed to understand the full consequences of their intervention on the debt issue at the Dacca meeting.

During the following months there were intensive negotiations between donors and Bangladesh on the debt issue, as is described in the following chapter. Irrespective of the results of the Dacca meeting, donors continued to express their strong preference for the formation of a consortium. There was a worsening of the balance of payments of Bangladesh during 1973–4, and by the middle of 1974, Bangladesh was in the throes of a food and foreign exchange crisis and desperately needed an immediate injection of foreign assistance. At this time, Bangladesh gave further thoughts to the idea of a consortium and decided to bend with the wind. The pressures had built up and time was running out. Needs must when the devil drives.[2]

The Pressures of Economic Exigence

Managing Bangladesh's external economy in the first few years of the country's existence was a continuous nightmare. Import requirements were far in excess of foreign exchange earnings; the ability to obtain adequate quantities of imported commodities and to plan these effectively depended on obtaining and utilising foreign aid as well as using Bangladesh's own resources. Programming imports proved to be a well nigh impossible task. The utilisation of non-project commodity assistance was slow. The administrative procedures of donors as well as those of Bangladesh impeded the flow of imports purchased under aid and there were also commercial difficulties. At times the shortage of imports was so acute and the uncertainties about future supplies so great that import programmes were established on a hand to mouth basis, and there were a number of occasions when emergency action was necessary as unpredictable changes threatened to drive Bangladesh into insolvency.

Re-establishing commercial links proved to be unexpectedly difficult. Oil was a case in point. Until March 1974, when the oil producing countries recognised Bangladesh, there was no direct contact with producers. The kind of crude oil needed to operate the one and only refinery was of a specification so finely drawn that it could be obtained only from one or two countries; Bangladesh's total consumption (only 1.2 million tons) was too small to be of much interest to major international oil exporting companies and there was in any case little contact with the oil market. The country, in consequence, came very near to running out of oil on a number of occasions.

The system of state trading operated badly and proved to have serious drawbacks in conditions of world market scarcity and rising prices. In 1973, prices of commodities on world markets rose steeply. Attempting to purchase commodities when prices were rising rapidly on the basis of international tender, as the trading corporation of Bangladesh was required to do, meant that Bangladesh frequently missed the boat and had to pay much more than would have been possible if spot purchases had been made. This was compounded by developing scarcities of such vital imports as cement, fertiliser, cotton and cotton yarn as prices rose steeply. Sometimes it seemed that goods could not be obtained at any price. It was known that Bangladesh's financial resources were slim and this ruled out any possibility of making long-term deals; shortage of resources also made it impossible to buy on advantageous terms when such opportunities presented themselves.

These problems might have been overcome if it had been

possible to establish and maintain substantial foreign exchange reserves. However this did not seem justified, the opportunity cost was too great when every dollars worth of imports was needed to keep things going, and at times prevent starvation. With no stocks to fall back on, the situation called for the most expert management of available foreign exchange resources. This was easier said than done. Such were the vagaries of fortune and the unpredictability of the situation that it was not always possible to keep foreign reserves to a minimum. There were times when they rose sharply and without intent. Accumulation of reserves did occur from time to time because of administrative delays in issuing import licences or in utilising them because of the inexperience of importers, both public and private, in making overseas contracts. It was found that there were often lags between opening letters of credit and making payments in respect of them, and that outstanding liabilities were frequently carried over from one shipping period to another. Frequently sellers failed to honour contracts as prices rose astronomically on world markets. There was no way of enforcing performance since sellers could pay the penalty for failing to fill the contract and still be much better off by selling elsewhere.

Better management of Bangladesh's foreign exchange resources would have improved the economic position of the economy in 1972 and 1973 but even the most efficient of administrative systems could not have resolved the underlying problems which were all too apparent by 1974. Annual import requirements at that time concentrated on essentials and, allowing for a very modest development programme, came to about $1400 million. Against this, commodity exports might be capable of bringing in $450 million per year. It was apparent that after meeting a deficit on invisibles something like $1000 million in foreign aid was needed to allow the economy to function with some semblance of efficiency. The planned volume of imports was no more than that of 1969–70, when the population was over 10 per cent less, and could not be regarded as excessive.

The country's finances were heavily in the red, the economic situation was black, and worse was to follow. In August 1974, there was one of the worst floods in twenty-five years with heavy damage to the rice crop, as well as some to standing jute. At about the same time there was an explosion, believed at the time to be due to sabotage, in the biggest fertiliser factory (capable of producing 360,000 tons of urea per year); this added further to import requirements. The additional bill for food and fertiliser was estimated to be about $200 million. Estimates of the balance of payments gap, not covered by financial resources in sight, were now in the region of $650 million.

As the economic crisis affecting the balance of payments worsened, there was an increasing realisation that Bangladesh's problems were not due solely to difficulties in adjusting from war to peace conditions, nor transient in nature. The underlying problem was one of scarcity of resources with which to develop. In the conditions prevailing, socially and politically as well as economically, Bangladesh had no real prospect of reducing its dependence on aid; substantial foreign assistance over many years was bound to be needed if living standards were to be improved significantly by the end of the century. It was not just to Bangladesh that this was apparent; donors, too, began to get a better appreciation of the position and to realise that if they were to help Bangladesh at all they had to give assistance in a big way. With the debt issue out of the way or nearly so, need and inclination were beginning to converge, and the desperate shortage of food apparent in mid-1974 gave urgency to the establishment of aid relationships on an organised and secure footing in a manner desired by major donors.

The opposition of Bangladesh to the formation of a consortium had receded in importance. The consortium began to be seen not as a substitute for bilateral discussions but as a supplement to them. Specific aid projects were not discussed at consortium meetings, let alone negotiated; a major function of an aid consortium was seen to be to provide an occasion for the pledging of further assistance by donors. There could be advantages to Bangladesh if she were present in such discussions. It was realised that the magnitude of aid required was such that it would be unlikely to be forthcoming unless donors were in a position to concert their actions and combine to exert common pressure to find the sums needed. Moreover, experience had shown that the absence of a consortium did not prevent donors from meeting together under the leadership of the World Bank either in Paris or for that matter in Dacca. Such meetings had been taking place frequently, quite apart from the exchanges that had centred on the debt issue.

The 1974 World Bank Economic Report

While these developments and manoeuvrings towards an organised aid group for Bangladesh took place in 1973 and 1974, the World Bank staff was heavily engaged in the preparation of a comprehensive economic review and analysis of Bangladesh. The Bank's work on this endeavour began after the First Five Year Plan became available in the summer of 1973. Previous World Bank reports had been prepared for Pakistan as a whole and were concerned with East Pakistan only in that context. In the meantime, a new country had been established and a new set of economic problems had emerged in consequence. Bangladesh was in the course of evolving its own social and economic policies, and while many of the things it would be necessary to do would be determined largely as a technical response to particular problems, it was necessary to give a new direction to events in line with the aspirations of the Government and people of the new country.

A full-scale review by the World Bank of events in Bangladesh since its creation and of the plans it had formed for the future was felt by donors to be very important. It would represent the first opportunity of the international community to appraise the situation through its own intermediaries. The impression created by the report would be instrumental in forming international opinion and paving the way for future relationships. Conscious of this, the Government made every effort to facilitate the visit of the mission that was to prepare the report and to devote attention to requests for explanation of Bangladesh's positions; and this at a time when the whole Government machine was greatly overburdened by the task of establishing secure and efficient government in the aftermath of war, and with rather too few administrators employed to carry out the task. The results of all these efforts were far from salutary.

From the point of view of establishing good relations between the Bank and Bangladesh and promoting understanding between Bangladesh and the international community, the draft report which emerged from the Bank turned out to be more conducive to discord than co-operation. Even where on substantive matters honest differences between the Bank and the Government were admitted, the Government felt that comments were made in unnecessarily denigrating language. The Government of Bangladesh was dismayed.

The greatest difficulties were raised by critical and sweeping generalisations about the administration and political leadership of the country. It seemed to the Government that the Bank was casting serious aspersions on its integrity. In the view of those writing for the Bank, it appeared as though scarcely a foreign exchange transaction took place that was not the subject of a rake-off by somebody in a position of power and able to salt funds away abroad. Corruption was judged to be of quite a different order of magnitude from that existing in the past, reflecting the declining real income of civil servants and the arbitrary role of political influence. The Government felt itself criticised for not having the capacity to do a decent job of official business, even defined in the narrowest sense; to organise the production of canned fruit, or the importation of tallow and the pricing of razor blades. Evident impatience was felt with the attempts of the Government to pursue a socialist policy which, as viewed from Washington, was not considered to result in a socially preferable pattern of income distribution, in part because there were no rewards for good performance and no punishments for ineptitude. The Plan prepared by Bangladesh was criticised as being devoid of individual programmes and projects that could be implemented, and even for not quite managing to disguise the lack of a clear central conception of where the economy was heading.

These and other sweeping generalisations were objected to by the Government; the tone of the report and the general attitude reflected were not felt to be those of a constructive partnership or friendly dialogue. Too much centred on failures; little attempt was made to highlight successes and achievements. Neither was any understanding shown of the severity of the obstacles that Bangladesh had had to overcome, nor of the extent to which natural calamities and the adverse external economic environment hampered economic recovery and thwarted efforts to get development going again. The prevalence of corruption had been recognised by the Government and referred to openly: to reiterate what had already been said without any suggestions based on some analysis as to how the situation might be remedied was, to say the least, unhelpful. The problem of corruption was not confined to Bangladesh; it occurs in varying degrees in developing and developed countries. Mere exhortation can do little to eliminate it; the Government might have accepted suggestions of legal and institutional measures needed to reduce it, but nothing was said on this point.

One of the unfortunate results of the bad impression made by the report was that it created great reluctance to give serious consideration to those parts that merited it. The report contained a number of valuable insights, not least those concerned with the rural economy. The Bank's analysis in earlier years of agriculture and water development as well as the policy recommendations that emerged from that work were highly regarded in Bangladesh. In these sectors thorough analysis had been followed by constructive criticisms which, although not always accepted, were given full consideration by planners in Bangladesh. Also the Bank's 1974 economic report dealt with the real issues of agriculture and the rural economy in an objective and instructed way; the pity was that the context of that analysis was such that it was impossible to use the report as a basis for a meeting of minds between Bangladesh and the donors.

As a document by itself, the World Bank Economic Report prepared by the Bank in 1973–4 may have been of little moment, but it came at a time and in a form which was not particularly helpful to Bangladesh and it strained rather than eased Bangladesh's relations with donors in general and the World Bank in particular. The experience of the Report gave fuel to the fire of suspicion that in any enterprise dominated by the World Bank there would be pressures amounting to little less than attempts to determine the country's economic policies from outside. With views as expressed in the Report, the credibility of the Bank as an aggressive leader in mobilising the very considerable economic assistance needed by Bangladesh was questioned. Would not such report writing discourage potential donors from granting substantial assistance to Bangladesh? Was there not the danger that they would conclude from the Bank's analysis that assistance could only be grossly misused or largely expropriated by greedy politicians aided by corrupt administrators and transferred abroad?

In response to the protest of the Bangladesh Government the draft report was marginally revised to make the wording more acceptable. But the damage lingered and could not readily be undone. The draft report, even with limited circulation, had in fact been made available quite generally throughout the international aid community and could only affect Bangladesh's relationship with donors adversely.

Formation of an Aid Group for Bangladesh

By mid-1974, Bangladesh felt compelled by necessity to submit itself to the aid donors. An aide-memoire was sent to all donors, drawing attention to the magnitude of the food and balance of payment crisis, and the reasons for it, and stressing the need for immediate assistance to meet payments on past commitments. Missions from Bangladesh were sent to explain the desperate need for assistance to donor countries and agencies. Predictably, a number of important donors suggested that this was the kind of situation in which they would like to consider what should be done in a common framework, in conjunction with other donors. The need for the immediate formation of a consortium for Bangladesh to mobilise assistance was pointed out. The role of the World Bank and the IMF in such a consortium was clearly indicated, when the UK and other governments requested that an 'independent' analysis and report on the economic situation, including the balance of payments prospects, be prepared in relation to both the short- and long-term problems of the Bangladesh economy.

In July 1974 the Government accepted the inevitable and requested the World Bank to constitute a consortium of aid donors for Bangladesh. Also the IMF was approached and asked to give short-term assistance and to send a mission to Bangladesh for consultations. At the same time major Western donors were also contacted individually and a request for an early meeting of a consortium conveyed to them. The Bangladesh initiative was well received and this paved the way for further action.

The worsening of the balance of payments crisis consequent on the heavy floods already described led Bangladesh to request the Bank to call an emergency meeting of the consortium in August to consider the immediate problem, and a regular meeting in October 1974 to consider medium-term requirements. In its response, the World Bank emphasised that the most important source of short-term cash assistance was the IMF and that an agreement with the Fund would be needed to gain access to the second and third credit tranches. The Bank warned Bangladesh against resorting in desperation to short-term commercial borrowing which would create a long-term debt problem, emphasised the need to keep the import bill to a minimum, and made it plain that it expected that an 'understanding' would be reached with the Fund. On this basis the Bank was ready to call an emergency meeting. The Bangladesh Government had already taken drastic measures to cut its import programme to include the barest minimum of fresh commitments, as outstanding liabilities were already in excess of available resources, and it fully intended to pursue policies that could eventually place the economy on a sound footing.

The emergency meeting was held in mid-August in Washington under the Chairmanship of the Bank and was attended by the major donors. The Bank submitted a note on Bangladesh's emergency requirements, and recommended immediate cash assistance to Bangladesh to enable it to meet outstanding liabilities of $200 million by the end of September 1974. It was argued by the Bank that the immediate reason for the crisis lay in the rapid deterioration that had taken place in Bangladesh's terms of trade in the last two years on a scale that no country could have expected to have surmounted in so short a time,[3] let alone a very low income country like Bangladesh which had no option, short of starvation, to make the required adjustments. The Bank concluded, therefore, that the only viable response to Bangladesh's difficulties lay in the immediate provision of cash by donors to finance imports on a scale that would allow the economy to be sustained at least at current levels of activity. It was not only purchases of grain, but also such essential items as petroleum and raw materials, which could not be imported either through available commodity aid or barter trade, which made the extraordinarily heavy claims on cash resources.

As advised, Bangladesh did in fact resort to the IMF by drawing the $37.5 million available as the second tranche of its quota, but did not reach agreement with the Fund to draw the third tranche until well into 1975. The proceeds of the second IMF tranche plus a further $35 million of short-term borrowing proved inadequate to meet the situation. As no other immediate emergency help commensurate with the need was forthcoming, the financial emergency was met in part by discounting export bills, deferring payments, and running down reserves to still lower levels. Even though donors did allow some use of commodity aid already in the pipeline to meet outstanding payments due to suppliers in their respective countries, the programmed minimum imports for the months of August, September and October had in part to be forgone. This included reductions in food imports in the remaining months of 1974 when there was famine and starvation, the worst since the Bengal famine of 1943.

The October 1974 Aid Group Meeting

The emergency meeting in Washington was followed by the first regular meeting of the Aid Group for Bangladesh in Paris in October 1974. The Bangladesh Government did not again raise the question of venue; it was considered of no significance in the context of what had happened in the preceding year. The Bank, under whose chairmanship the Aid Group Meeting was to be placed, circulated a strong plea for substantial foreign assistance to Bangladesh in view of her short-term needs, caused by natural calamity and adverse external economic factors; it also recognised that in view of the poverty of domestic resources, Bangladesh would continue to need substantial foreign assistance in the future for sustained development. Indeed, the Bank's position raised the prospect of a new approach to the problems of Bangladesh, with the donors being asked to give the country a chance to survive the immediate crisis and an opportunity to move progressively towards development.

During the weeks prior to the Meeting, consultations had taken place with the Bank and major donors who again had raised a number of issues of policy and planning which had been subjects of frequent and long discussions over the preceding two years. The Government was urged to reach early decisions on such matters in order to be able to record positive policies and measures for their implementation at the Meeting. The Bank further advised Bangladesh to emphasise its potential for development, so that the participating countries should not feel that it would remain a continuous drain on other countries' resources – even though the Aid Group was meeting in the context of a severe balance of payment crisis, aggravated by floods and an explosion in the biggest fertiliser factory.

The Bank's major Economic Report had been available in

draft form to the donors for some time, and the major donors felt that it provided a suitable basis for discussions by the Aid Group. This Bank Report had pointed out that there was little or no difference between the Bangladesh Plan and itself in terms either of analysis of policies and institutional changes required for growth or of recommendations for action. The main difference between the two was in terms of the projection of resources, foreign and domestic, which determined the size of the Plan, and there were also some not very significant differences about sectoral priorities.[4] It is remarkable that in spite of identity of views on policy packages and institutional changes between the Bank Report and the Plan, the donors referred to the Bank Report for guidance on changes in policies and institutions and not to the Plan.

Bangladesh prepared documentation for the Meeting in the form of a memorandum on the current economic situation and prospects, with projections of resources, investment and foreign assistance requirements for 1974–5, and a report on the latest status of aid commitments and disbursement by types and sources of assistance. The Bank, as usual, also prepared a document on the current situation and prospects giving the assessment of the foreign assistance required for the following year.

Although estimates of the required level of commitment of aid differed, it was evident that more than $1000 million was needed. Ultimately, the amount of aid pledged in 1974/5 was to build up to $1.2 billion, but the actual commitment at the meeting was disappointing; only about one-third of the total was forthcoming as pledges. This led to discussions about the need to speed up aid disbursements by improving administrative arrangements. It was agreed that one way to do this was to hold periodic meetings on the question, particularly between World Bank and Bangladesh representatives. There were a great many aspects that could be considered for improvement, including attempts to shorten the time needed for project identification, feasibility studies, project preparation and implementation.

The IMF, while agreeing with the identification of the critical policy issues as described by the Bank, dwelt at length and in great details on its own particular area of specialisation, which included export policy, smuggling and simplification of the import control regimes. It added that in order to overcome the crisis and to lay the basis for steady development, Bangladesh required large-scale assistance of a kind capable of being put to timely and productive use and on terms suited to its particular circumstances. At the same time, it stressed that the authorities needed to make major adjustments over a wide range of economic and financial policies; without these, foreign assistance would not yield the desired results.

In fact, the recurrent theme in the meeting was the exchange rate policy of Bangladesh and the need for an early devaluation. Once this issue was introduced into the discussion, all the other representatives followed in emphasising the critical need for devaluation.[5] There was considerable criticism also of other economic policies currently being pursued, which it was felt jeopardised the future by critical failures in economic management.

For bilateral donors, besides the policies pressed by the World Bank and the Fund, the most prominent issues were concerned with agricultural development and special programmes for the improvement of the conditions of the rural poor, including the role of local government institutions, co-operatives and extension services. Some countries pledged food aid on the understanding that Bangladesh would seek to direct the food to the poorest sections of the population, and procure domestically an increasing amount to meet the requirements of the public distribution system. A few countries emphasised the role of small-scale industry and others welcomed the recent revision of the industrial policy by the Government of Bangladesh which gave a greater role to private enterprise. There was reference to the underutilisation of existing productive capacity and to inefficiencies in foreign trade and the import licencing system.

Not all delegations wished to intervene actively in the economic and political scene in Bangladesh. The point was put that the problem of organising the people of Bangladesh, so as to release the productive capacity of the country, was one for the people and leaders of Bangladesh and not a suitable subject of discussion at a consortium meeting.

In general, however, donors expressed a remarkable degree of unanimity of opinion both in accepting the Bank's analysis of the economic ills of Bangladesh and in accepting its leadership. They recognised that the economic policies and actions required were matters for political decision making by the Government of Bangladesh, but did not hesitate to point out the likely consequences of courses of action different from those they proposed, based as they were on a broad range of experience round the world, which should be relied upon by Bangladesh to avoid some of the failures of economic and social management and development policy.

There were in fact considerable differences exposed in the economic philosophies of Bangladesh and most of the donors. Rightly or wrongly, the countries of the Indian sub-Continent have chosen to regulate their economies in a large measure by the operation of controls. Many studies of the operations of such controls have shown that they may lead to inefficiencies and, from some points of view, also to a maldistribution of resources, but it is scarcely realistic to expect, as some donors seem to do, that they are likely to be removed by external urging to rely on market mechanisms and private initiative. Nor can it be assumed that countries need reports from the Bank or the IMF to draw their attention to deficiencies in their fiscal or monetary policies.

The desire of the donors, of the Aid Group, and of the World Bank and the Fund to influence policy formation in Bangladesh was clearly demonstrated in the form and content of the proceedings at this first Aid Group Meeting. Power without responsibility is not an exercise to be lightly indulged in and attempts to intervene in other countries' affairs is generally resented. Yet it may be true that without some such opportunity to make observations on the affairs of aid-receiving countries, and to hear their reply to criticism, donors would feel that they were not fulfilling their duty to express their legitimate concern about how assistance is used.

Normalisation of Relationships; The June 1975 Aid Group Meeting

The major theme on which the donors concentrated in their meeting in Dacca in March 1973 had been the sharing of Pakistan's debt liability; in the formal Aid Group Meeting in October 1974 it was the adjustment of the exchange rate; in June 1975 the attention of donors was more widely spread. The devaluation which had taken place in May 1975 was regarded as an important step in the right direction and this impressed the donors as evidence of good intentions. At least as important was the improvement in the economic situation that had taken place between the two meetings. General despondency and despair in the country had subsided; starvation, so evident in 1974, had receded, mainly because of good harvests but partly also because of improvements in carrying out the food programmes. The trade relation with Cuba had been effectively broken so as to ease aid relations with the United States. Commitments from all sources had built up over the year to a total of about $1.2 billion and two-thirds of this was in the form of food and commodities.

In other respects also progress had been made. The Government was being more decisive about its economic policies. Monetary management was being pressed and with the increase in output, prices had fallen from previous excessive levels. There had been a demonetisation of the 100 Tk notes as part of deflationary measures. At the same time action was under way to reformulate the First Five Year Plan or at least to screen and re-order the priorities of development projects within that Plan in the light of new price and cost relationships, both domestic and foreign. A revised programme for the remaining three years of the Plan period was nearing completion by the time of the June 1975 Aid Group Meeting. The principal measures undertaken by the Government following the last meeting were described in the Bangladesh memorandum circulated before the meeting. They related to food procurement, pricing policy, attempts at co-ordination and the supervision of aid, improved procedures for aid disbursement and the establishment of the Project Implementation Bureau in the Office of the President.

Some aspects of the changes in policies which had been made appealed particularly to the dominant members of the Aid Group: the greater emphasis on market mechanisms, as well as the concentration of political and administrative power that was expressed in the assumption of a presidential system of government and evident in the attendant changes in the power of the administration. As usual, the need for further action and supporting measures was urged by donors, and emphasis placed on the creation of an appropriate framework for the effective use of aid to further economic growth. In keeping with earlier meetings, donors proffered advice and stressed the urgency of reform and efficiency of economic, financial and administrative operations.

The IMF recounted the need for measures of credit control,

including the need to control deficit financing, and to give special attention to the requirements of the agricultural sector and import trade. The importance of reducing subsidies and increasing revenues through realistic pricing by nationalised enterprises and improvement in managerial efficiency was described as a means to increase resource mobilisation. The World Bank highlighted three areas: domestic procurement and distribution of food (including successful anti-smuggling measures), population planning, and speeding up aid disbursement. The distribution of food under the rationing system continued to attract attention. The Government was urged to reduce the food subsidy; to concentrate on the needs of the poorest sections of the community; to increase procurement at prices attractive to farmers. In some respects these observations were a prelude to questions about the Government's projected requirement of 5 millions tons of imported food over the next three years. The Bangladesh Government pressed for support to establish a reserve stock of 750,000 tons of foodgrain in order to be better able to stabilise the price of food. While devaluation would tend to increase food prices, larger imports and a reserve stock would help to contain pressures. Increased food supplies were also necessary for labour intensive rural projects in the villages within the 'food for work' programme.

The efficiency of the internal distribution system for fertilizer also came in for discussion. It was felt that Bangladesh's proposal that a system of compulsory co-operatives should be introduced in all the villages needed clarification. A changeover from the existing system of co-operatives, with which Bangladesh had long experience and the donors were familiar and were engaged in financing, was thought to run the risk of causing dislocation, unless well thought out and implemented in stages.

Exports of jute and other commodities were also considered, because the Bank had argued that some export targets were too low. A role for the private sector in the export of raw jute in competition with public sector export co-operatives was urged. The discussion passed to the management of the nationalised industries, including relations between the Government and nationalised industries. The lack of trained personnel at the lower level of administration and management was believed to be a great stumbling block not only in nationalised industries but for every aspect of the economy, including the utilisation of foreign aid. Proposals to improve the administration of population control dwelt on the participation of female workers in the Government's family planning programmes, which was far from satisfactory and fell well short of the Government's own targets. From Bangladesh's point of view the most important discussions were concerned with the magnitude and composition of aid. The Bangladesh Government and the World Bank both estimated the requirements of new commitments of foreign assistance for the year 1975–6 at about $1200 million, which in terms of disbursement during that year would mean about $800 million; in addition, the disbursement from the pipeline was expected to be $400 million or somewhat more. In fact, new commitments made during the consortium meeting reached nearly $1000 million. It was argued that aid commitments needed to be predominantly in the form of food and commodity assistance and donors were in fact able to go a long way to meet this need.

By the summer of 1975, Bangladesh had carried out a re-examination of the strategies being following in the area of social and economic organisation and management. The devaluation of the Taka, the declaration of the growth of population as a major national problem, reductions in subsidies on food and fertiliser, import liberalisation and greater emphasis on the private sector of the economy in the middle of 1976 had the effect of bringing policies more into line with the ideologies and practices of major Western aid donors and international institutions. Bangladesh had also accepted the role apparently expected of her by the internationaid community of an attentive and accommodating supplicant of assistance. With the Aid Group Meeting in June 1975, therefore, the stage was set for the conduct of policies in Bangladesh, which found favour with donors, and for general relationships with bilateral and multilateral aid agencies, which were likely to be more free of friction. The interplay of aid and influence in Bangladesh is still, in 1979, following these lines.

Notes

1. The pros and cons of reliance on foreign aid in general and on a Western Aid consortium as debated in Bangladesh in 1972 are described in Chapter 2.
2. This is written ''tis true; I have seen it. I assure you, that at master Gaster's command, the very heavens tremble, and all the earth shakes: his command is

called, Do this or die. Needs must when the Devil drives, there's no gainsaying of it' (*The Works of Rabelais*, translated from the French by Gustav Doré, printed for private circulation, Nottingham, Book IV, chapter 57, p. 513).

3. The Bangladesh Government estimated at the time that a 74 per cent increase in import prices took place between 1972–3 and 1974–5. More recent estimations based on 'current weighting' suggest that the increase was over 100 per cent.
4. A smaller size Plan, given the objectives prescribed, would have resulted in a sectoral allocation very nearly as suggested by the Bank Report.
5. The role of the IMF and the Aid Group in the decision to devalue the Bangladesh Taka is discussed in Chapter 11.

9 The Debt Liability of Pakistan

JUST FAALAND

The dramatic developments in 1971 as they unfolded within Bangladesh: the contrast in attitudes and actions of the USA and the USSR, the special role played by India, the diversity of experience of Bangladesh's own leaders and of the population at large, conditioned the positions taken by the Government of the new state and limited its room for manoeuvre. Pakistan was regarded with bitterness and it seemed unlikely that good relations could be quickly established. Considerations of politics and economics were closely intertwined.

The story of the resolution of the issue of external debt liability accumulated by Pakistan prior to the division of the country in 1971, can be understood only in relation to its political ramifications. The story has intrinsic interest as part of the political and economic history of the two countries most closely concerned. It also serves to illustrate the weight and modes of pressures of external interests, including in particular the World Bank, on an economically weak developing country.

In December 1971, the accumulated outstanding debt liability of the old Pakistan amounted to about US$3 billion equivalents. The corresponding total value of external assets was never established in the same detail. They included subscriptions to international agencies, in particular the International Monetary Fund, which these agencies allowed the truncated Pakistan to retain as exclusively its own without seeking Bangladesh's agreement or even deigning to consult her. Throughout its negotiations with creditors on the settlement of the debt issue, Bangladesh insisted that this was a matter eventually to be resolved between her and Pakistan bilaterally, as part of an overall agreement on relations between the two countries and, specifically, that it had to be considered together with the issue of the settlement of assets.[1] The creditors led by the World Bank did not accept this tenet of Bangladesh. As a result, for a period of more than two years the Pakistan debt settlement became a central issue in the evolution of relations between Bangladesh and the major countries of the Western World. As other bilateral issues of conflict between Bangladesh and Pakistan were resolved, in particular the crucial question of the Pakistani prisoners of war held in India, and as the pressures of creditors on an economically weakening debtor persisted and mounted, Bangladesh yielded and eventually accepted the separation of the problems of Pakistan's external debt from other issues of relations between the two countries.

The account and analysis in this chapter of negotiations on the question of Bangladesh's accepting a part of Pakistan's debt liability throws light on a number of interrelated issues. First, it provides a case study of the problems involved in the division of external debt liabilities of a country when a part of it emerges as an independent state through a war of liberation. There are few parallels of this sort in contemporary history and the Bangladesh case is unique. The issue of the division of external debt liability between Pakistan and Bangladesh must also be distinguished from the problem of cancellation or rescheduling of debt of a developing country faced with balance of payments difficulties and resource shortages. Second, it illustrates the power and leverage that can be exerted by external creditors, including international financial institutions, and in particular the World Bank, in the process of negotiations on debt issues, and explains why Bangladesh had ultimately to accept a part of the external debt liability. What is important here is not so much the concepts and principles of the division of the debt burden, as the procedures and methods of negotiation which were employed by the creditors in making Bangladesh accept a part of the debt liability. Third, it illustrates the considerations which governed the determination of the terms on which the debt liability was to be repaid. In 1971, when the war of liberation of Bangladesh was underway, Pakistan unilaterally imposed a moratorium on debt service payments on its outstanding external debt. During the war (March to December 1971) no new aid or loan agreements were made, but existing loans and credits were not discontinued.[2] In

May 1972, the creditors jointly agreed to reschedule Pakistan's debt until June 1973; the period covered by the rescheduling arrangement included the year of default, 1971, with retroactive effect and without penalty.

Early in 1972, the creditors raised the issue of Bangladesh's share in the past debt liability of Pakistan. As the donors gradually moved away from giving grants for rehabilitation and reconstruction towards development assistance, the issue of liability for the past debt was stressed more and more. It was during this period that Bangladesh applied for membership of the IMF and the World Bank. This gave the Bank the opportunity to take the lead in raising the issue of past debt liability with Bangladesh and to act as a spokesman for all the creditors. Before the middle of 1972, the Bank told Bangladesh that the creditors were engaged in collecting information, from their own records, on the division of Pakistan's pre-1971 debt liability between the two countries. The creditors in turn also requested Pakistan to provide information and data bearing on the division of the liability. The Bank informed Bangladesh that the statistical work on the division of the debt liability would enable Bangladesh to get an idea of the order of magnitude involved and to formulate its own ideas on the subject for future action at an appropriate time. This activity on the part of the Bank was not undertaken in response to any request by Bangladesh, but independently and on its own initiative. Apart from the Bank, the bilateral donors who were the first to raise the issue of the past debt liability with Bangladesh were the Governments of the USA, the Federal Republic of Germany and France. Their respective shares in outstanding loans to Pakistan ranked in that order, the French credit being the least significant.

As soon as possible after the establishment of Bangladesh, negotiations were started with donors for the revival and reactivation of ongoing projects – those which were started before the war but remained uncompleted. Bangladesh wanted to revive investment activity as early as possible and the quickest way to do so was to review ongoing projects. Since Bangladesh did not have the resources to do this herself, it was necessary to negotiate with those who had originally undertaken to finance the individual projects with the intention of making new agreements. As part of the process of reactivation, Bangladesh agreed to accept liability for past investments already made by the creditors in those projects which were to be restarted. In many cases, the total cost of completion had escalated due to increases in prices and other factors, and it was necessary to increase the amount of credit above that originally made available. Accordingly, new credit agreements were made for higher amounts but in many cases under more liberal terms and conditions than those originally agreed.

Bangladesh attempted to devise a definition of ongoing projects as far as it was logically conceivable. The definition was liberal; in practice all projects in which past investments had not led to the actual commissioning of the projects, were defined as ongoing, irrespective of the amount of additional investment involved.[3] In some cases, the additional investment required was very small and in a few cases, only additional technical and engineering consultancy service from the original contractors was needed for the projects to be activated. Such technical services were essential and were only available from the original suppliers of equipment, who were to be paid for their service under the original loan agreements.

The fact that Bangladesh accepted liability for past disbursements on ongoing projects, even though the terms and conditions of repayment were negotiated under new agreements with the creditors, was construed by the creditors of Pakistan to mean that Bangladesh had accepted the principle that debts incurred for projects physically located in Bangladesh were the responsibility of Bangladesh. This was a misreading of the situation; the choice of which projects to activate had been Bangladesh's. There was no obligation on the part of Bangladesh automatically to reactivate all ongoing projects and enter into new credit agreements, incorporating past investments. Moreover, in a number of cases reactivation had been arranged with the help of grants, which obviated the need to make a new loan agreement. In these cases the question of accepting liability for past investments did not have to be discussed.

By March 1973, the pressure exerted by the creditors on Bangladesh mounted; their rescheduling arrangement with Pakistan for the liability of the entire pre-1971 debt was due to expire by June 1973. Bangladesh was informed by them that Pakistan had stated that as from June 1973 she would refuse to service that portion of the pre-1971 debt, which she considered a liability of Bangladesh. Pakistan, the creditors further informed

Bangladesh, had already submitted to them a statement of the division of the debt liability between the two countries which included both project and non-project assistance. According to Pakistan's estimates about one-third of the total outstanding debt of slightly more than US$3 billion belonged to Bangladesh.

There was no reason why the creditors should accept Pakistan's proposal. In law the debt liabilities were those of Pakistan; the creditors could have insisted that she should continue to carry the entire debt burden. It was extremely unlikely that Pakistan, in spite of her stand, would have defaulted if it was made clear to her that such an action would result in the stoppage of all aid to her. The amount she would have lost by this would have far outweighed the cost of acknowledging the whole of the debt liability, which would almost certainly have been rescheduled.

The creditors did not vigorously and persistently seek to resolve the debt issue in this way; they preferred to exert the main pressure on Bangladesh to accept liability for a part of the pre-1971 debt. Bangladesh was overwhelmingly dependent on aid for the urgent task of rehabilitation and reconstruction and her bargaining strength was very weak. The common position which the creditors had established by March 1973 was relayed to the Government of Bangladesh by the World Bank in the following terms:

(i) The creditors were unwilling to accept any default on past debt; all the accumulated debt without exception must be borne by either Pakistan or Bangladesh.

(ii) The creditors had no interest in any particular division of liabilities and would accept any allocation of debt between the two countries, which were mutually agreed upon by them.

(iii) The creditors were not willing to suffer the consequences of any dispute between the two countries regarding the division of liability. Any interruption in the flow of debt service payments would affect adversely the credit worthiness of *both* the countries and not just Pakistan.

(iv) In bilateral negotiations between the two countries, any attempt by either party to introduce such factors as the flow of resources or transfer of assets between the two parts of Pakistan before 1971, would be treated by the donors as introducing 'extraneous factors'. If the in-

> troduction of such extraneous factors substantially delayed or jeopardised the outcome of negotiations, this would be treated by the donors as an unreasonable attitude on the part of the country concerned.

Though couched in terms of either country raising extraneous considerations, the last condition was mainly directed towards Bangladesh; it was Bangladesh which was insisting that the division of external debt should not be discussed without reference to the division of assets and to the methods of financing the formation of such assets. It was clear that the creditors had decided that Bangladesh must agree to carry a part of the external debt and that she must agree to a division of debt without reference to the division of the total assets of Pakistan at the time of independence between the two parts of Pakistan.

In international law, Bangladesh was under no obligation to accept Pakistan's debt liability. In the absence of an agreement with the creditors, it is generally accepted that a state that loses even a substantial part of its territory remains liable for all debt contracted prior to that loss. The old state does not have the right of attribution of its outstanding debt against the new state: Jordan paid debt service on projects located in territories occupied by Israel; Malaysia paid debt services on loans in public utilities located in Singapore. Most of the cases of debt succession in the past were settled by agreement between the countries concerned. This was the case between India and Pakistan, when two new states emerged in 1947, consequent on the dissolution of united British India. There is no universally accepted rule for the division of external liabilities but it has usually formed part of negotiations for the division of total assets and liabilities. The creditors had no legal authority and no precedent for demanding repayment from Bangladesh. The fact that no reduction had been made in Pakistan's capital subscription to the Fund and the Bank, where she retained full membership, was further evidence of her continued responsibility for established external financial matters. In her dealings with international organisations and other states, Pakistan, even after the loss of Bangladesh and a majority of the total population, considered herself, and was considered by others, as still continuing the identity of pre-1971 Pakistan.

Bangladesh's position was that even though she had no legal obligation to accept liability for external debts, she would do so if it formed part of a general settlement of the total external assets and liabilities of Pakistan. It was not enough to match liabilities for foreign debt against assets created by foreign credit in Bangladesh: the total flow of resources between the two parts of Pakistan, the ways in which resources had been used, and the ownership of the assets created had also to be taken into consideration. Bangladesh argued that, on balance, she had transferred substantial resources to Pakistan during the major part of the period she was united with Pakistan. It followed that Bangladesh's responsibility for servicing debt should be reduced to the extent that she had in fact aided Pakistan. Another factor to be taken into account was that Bangladesh suffered considerable damage and destruction in the war that Pakistan waged against her. The amount of this was estimated at over US$1 500 million. It was felt by Bangladesh entirely unjust that she should be required by the creditors to accept a part of the external debt liability, without any attempt to consider the whole question of the division of assets and liabilities between the two countries.

Bangladesh understood the concern of the creditors that an attempt to achieve a complete settlement of the financial issues in dispute between herself and Pakistan could take a long time and that an insistence on this being achieved first could delay the settlement of the claims of the creditors indefinitely. But by insisting on a separate settlement of the external debt liability, the creditors were really absolving Pakistan of any urgent need to enter into negotiations with Bangladesh. An immediate settlement of the debt issue would weaken the bargaining strength of Bangladesh in any future negotiations with Pakistan. Pakistan, being in physical possession of the lion's share of the assets created before 1971 as part of the development of Pakistan, to which Bangladesh was a major contributor, was under no pressure to enter into negotiations with Bangladesh and had little incentive to do so. The creditors' proposal to relieve Pakistan of part of the debt service was a partisan act and did nothing to encourage Pakistan to come to an agreement about the sharing of assets and liabilities. Had the creditors strictly observed the principal of legal obligation, they would have kept up the pressure on the legal borrower, Pakistan. It did not matter in such circumstances that the rescheduling of debt on generous terms and the promise of further aid to come was offered – though only as expressions of general intention – as an inducement to accepting some of Pakistan's debt liability. Such interchanges are generally not acceptable if matters of principle are at stake. Nor could Bangladesh allow the argument that the total ultimate debt liability would be reduced if it were put on Bangladesh, a poor country, (likely to be given favourable rescheduling terms) rather than on Pakistan, a relatively rich country, to sway the day. In linking Bangladesh's acceptance of past liabilities to the future flow of aid, creditors were bullying a country desperately dependent upon external assistance.

As described in Chapter 8, the Government of Bangladesh invited donors to an International Conference on the Development of Bangladesh, in Dacca at the end of March 1973. The Conference did not have the question of past debt liability on the agenda; its objectives were to review the progress of reconstruction and rehabilitation, to discuss the future programmes for development and to ascertain what financial commitment the donors might be prepared to make in 1973–4 for future development. There was no reason to raise the debt liability issue at the Conference itself as the Bangladesh Government had discussed it with the countries concerned.

Taking advantage of the presence of donor delegations in Dacca, a cabinet sub-committee, consisting of the Finance Minister (in the Chair), the Foreign Minister and the Deputy Chairman, Bangladesh Planning Commission, had been established to discuss the problems of the pre-1971 debt with the donors. The leaders of the delegations to the Conference met the cabinet sub-committee in a special meeting outside the Conference. Here the position and the point of view of the Bangladesh Government on the problem of past liability were explained in detail. The basic point made by Bangladesh was that it was politically unacceptable and too soon for her to consider accepting a part of the past debt liability of Pakistan. Pakistan had not recognised Bangladesh as an independent sovereign nation and the constitution of Pakistan still proclaimed Bangladesh as a part of its own territory. In all international affairs Pakistan continued to act as if Bangladesh was still part of Pakistan. Only when Pakistan recognised Bangladesh as an independent state would it be possible for Bangladesh to enter into negotiations about external liabilities.

The opportunity for a full discussion of the debt issue with the cabinet sub-committee having been taken and the clarification of the Government's position having already been received, the creditors nevertheless, as we have seen, were not prepared to keep to the agenda and comply with the request of the Government of Bangladesh to refrain from a discussion of the debt issue at the Conference itself. It was evident that the meetings of the World Bank sponsored consortium for Pakistan in 1972 and early 1973 had provided an opportunity for the creditors to meet and co-ordinate their approach to Bangladesh on the issue of past debt and that they were not prepared to lose any opportunity to exert pressure on Bangladesh. Virtually all donors raised the question at the Conference. They went further, insisting that development grants and credits for the next financial year would be conditional on Bangladesh's agreeing to accept a part of Pakistan's debt liability, the exact amount to be negotiated with the creditors.

The reaction of the creditors, after the failure of their pressures at the Dacca meeting to get Bangladesh to accept part of the external debt liability was not to insist that Pakistan shoulder the burden. Instead, under the leadership of the Bank, they decided to reschedule the debt service payments for another year until June 1974. The Government of Pakistan had made a public declaration that Pakistan from June 1973 onwards would cease to service debt that she regarded as the obligation of Bangladesh. The creditors by postponing debt service payments, prevented Pakistan, the legal borrower, from defaulting. For many of the creditors, their own legal requirement stipulated drastic action against a defaulting country. In this case such requirements did not apply to Bangladesh, for she could not be declared as being in default, according to the law of the creditor countries.

After the Dacca meeting, the Government of Bangladesh alerted its embassies on the need to bring the complex political and economic problems relating to the debt issues to the notice of the political authorities of the creditor countries and to do so at a considerably higher level than that of the officials who had been present at the Dacca meeting. The feeling in Dacca was that the aid and treasury officials at the meeting might have been overzealous and might have exceeded, if not the letter, at least the spirit, of the 'briefs' which they carried from their respective capitals. The Bangladesh Government wished to explain its position directly to the political authorities in the creditor countries. The ambassadors of Bangladesh were instructed to explain the entire circumstances surrounding the Dacca meeting;

in particular, they were to stress that Bangladesh regarded the attempt on the part of the donors to use the offer of development assistance as an instrument for influencing the settlement of a political issue with Pakistan as improper and unwarranted. The ambassadors were to confirm that when Pakistan was prepared to meet Bangladesh at a conference table as a sovereign and equal nation, Bangladesh would not countenance an indefinite prolongation of negotiations on the debt issue, since it appreciated the creditors' anxiety to secure a settlement of their claims. The same instructions were conveyed to the Executive Director representing Bangladesh at the World Bank.

Some softening of attitudes of individual donor governments soon became evident. The difficulty of making further progress in the face of the firm and publicly declared positions of Bangladesh and Pakistan was recognised by donors. More important, it now seemed to be realised that the consortium countries had been taking a short-sighted view of the problem at the Dacca meeting in March in their ostensible efforts to avoid impending default and its possible consequences. Donors might also have judged that the time would come in the near future when Bangladesh would have no option but to do as the creditors wished, and that relations between Bangladesh and Pakistan would return to a point permitting the debt settlement to be dealt with in a more general and less isolated and politically charged manner.

The World Bank was aware and concerned that in the process of the negotiation its credibility had been tarnished; it officially assured the Government of Bangladesh that the President of the Bank would do everything possible to help the country and that the unfortunate events of the Dacca conference should be best forgotten.[4] The willingness of the Bank to modify its approach, when it realised it was on a wrong tack, did much to improve relationships that had become very strained. It was against this background that the Bank sent a letter to creditors urging the postponement of the disputed debt service payments. In fact, by June 1973, the creditors had decided to reschedule the debt for another year. In July 1973, agreement was reached in Paris between the creditors and Pakistan with the following provisions relating to the debt liability issue:

(i) Pakistan would not be asked to accept liability for 'projects visibly located in Bangladesh' after June 1974.

(ii) In the meanwhile, Bangladesh would be persuaded to accept liability for these projects.
(iii) The conditional pledges for development assistance made to Bangladesh during the Dacca Conference of March 1973 would be made unconditional.
(iv) New commitments for the period following July 1974 would be conditional upon progress made by Bangladesh in accepting liability for projects located in Bangladesh.
(v) The identification of projects visibly located in Bangladesh would be subject to negotiation between creditors and Pakistan.

The provisions of this Agreement were informally, and later officially, conveyed to Bangladesh. Bangladesh had now to decide whether she should pursue her earlier policy of not accepting liability for any part of the pre-1971 debt and face a withdrawal of new aid and a growing bitterness in relationships with the creditors, who had generously assisted Bangladesh since her independence, or accept an obligation to service projects visibly located in Bangladesh. The acceptance of liability for such projects would force Bangladesh to retract its position that external debt could only be considered as a part of an overall settlement of all the assets and liabilities of Pakistan. Between July and September 1973 there was an agonising appraisal of the situation in the context of Bangladesh's very heavy dependence on external creditors. Bangladesh under international pressure had already withdrawn a number of political claims on Pakistan, including trials for war crimes. The creditors all along assured Bangladesh that they would be generous in the determination of the terms of repayment for the liability which Bangladesh would agree to accept. She eventually agreed to negotiate with the creditors about the 'visibly located projects' and in mid-September 1973, the following aide-memoire was sent to the creditors:

'The Government of the People's Republic of Bangladesh has examined the agreed minutes of the meeting of representatives of the member countries of the Pakistan's Consortium relating to Pakistan's external debt, dated July 31, 1973.

The Government of Bangladesh has noted that the member

countries had met to consider the situation arising out of "the unresolved problem of an equitable allocation of the total external debt of Pakistan". It has also been noted that the member countries considered that the legal liability for all the debts remained with the contracting party, namely Pakistan, and that the task of allocating the total external debt should be borne by the Governments of Pakistan and Bangladesh, and that any such allocation would be acceptable to the creditor governments.

The problem of equitable allocation of the total debt of Pakistan remains unresolved due to Pakistan's continued failure to negotiate with Bangladesh on the basis of sovereign equality. Bangladesh has consistently reaffirmed its readiness to work out an equitable solution of this problem through negotiations with Pakistan on the basis of sovereign equality.

The Bangladesh Government has, however, taken note of the anxiety expressed by the creditors to pursue the matter of projects described as "visibly located in Bangladesh".

Without prejudice to the position stated above, and to Bangladesh's claims on Pakistan, Bangladesh is ready to enter into negotiations with the countries and agencies concerned with regard to projects completed before independence which fall within the description "visibly located in Bangladesh."'

The Paris Agreement of July 1973 had not mentioned the subject of outstanding liabilities for commodity and food assistance received prior to the establishment of Bangladesh. Its silence on the subject could mean that the subject was kept in abeyance for the time being and could be raised again at a time considered suitable by creditors; in other words, that the creditors kept their options open and would decide on this subject depending upon how negotiations on the visibly located projects progressed. Alternatively, the absence of reference to liabilities for food aid and commodity assistance could imply that Bangladesh was absolved of any such liability and that Pakistan would remain fully responsible for these credits. Bangladesh proceeded on this latter assumption.

Even though the Paris Agreement had explicitly stipulated that conditionality of pledges of assistance imposed by creditors in March 1973 would be lifted, donors did not follow a uniform policy in this respect. While the USA, the Netherlands and

Belgium on their own initiative lifted conditionality straight away, Canada, France, Italy and the UK kept silent on the subject and did not lift conditionality until they had received the aide-memoire of the Government of Bangladesh in mid-September 1973. Japan went one step further in demanding a separate written undertaking.[5] In all cases, however, negotiations for new aid agreements proceeded simultaneously with the negotiation relating to the assumption of liability for projects 'visibly located' in Bangladesh.

The World Bank asserted that it was not a party to the general agreements made with the creditors; it considered its loans and credits outside the purview of the Paris Agreement, and claimed the status of a preferred creditor in the sense that it would neither write off nor reschedule any of its credits. The Bank took the position that its procedure must be simply to present to both countries what the Bank itself, in its wisdom and in the light of the best evidence available, considered to be an equitable division of the entire outstanding debt, and to seek agreement with Bangladesh to take over liability for the portion which in the Bank's own judgement had been disbursed for the benefit of the territory which subsequently became Bangladesh.

According to the strict interpretation of the Paris Agreement, Pakistan was absolved of the liability for Bangladesh projects, after June 1974, even if at that time or later Bangladesh refused to accept the liability for them. In other words, absolving Pakistan from liability for such projects was not conditional upon Bangladesh's acceptance of liability; in the extreme case therefore, there could be loans for which there would be no country accepting liability. The Bank insisted that this was not acceptable for any of its own loans and credits. Moreover, although there was nothing in the Bank's Charter which prevented its participation in rescheduling arrangements, it refused to consider such action, ostensibly because this would adversely affect the Bank's creditworthiness in the international capital markets. Bangladesh, in its turn, pointed out that this argument – whatever its merits in respect of World Bank loans – did not apply to IDA to which most of the disputed credits belonged. In any event, the Bank did not borrow from the private capital markets in the same way as other private credit institutions; its borrowings were guaranteed by its member governments who individually were ready to accept rescheduling arrangements.

At a more fundamental level, Bangladesh pointed out that even if the status of preferred creditor were granted to the Bank (both IDA and IBRD), it should apply to her relationship with Pakistan, who was the legal borrower, and should not affect the Bank's relationships with Bangladesh. In any case, Pakistan had in fact serviced all of Pakistan's pre-1971 debt owed to the World Bank and IDA; by the same reasoning in respect to the projects on which Bangladesh and the Bank might not come to an agreement, the Bank had the option, if indeed it were a preferred creditor, to go back to Pakistan and continue to insist on debt service there.

The Bank in fact went even further in its pressures on Bangladesh. It extended its interpretation of the 'preferred creditor' status to include not only liability for 'projects visibly located' in Bangladesh but also, and equally, liability for commodity aid to Pakistan as far as it happened to have been unloaded in East Pakistan ports. If this had been accepted by Bangladesh, it would have raised a whole range of complicated issues as to how commodity credits made by the Bank to Pakistan should be apportioned, including the question of what part of them could really be construed as having benefited Bangladesh and what part Pakistan.[6] In the various aide-memoires that Bangladesh submitted to the creditors, including the one in which she agreed to negotiate on projects visibly located in Bangladesh, no distinction was made between the Bank and the other creditors. The Government saw no reason why liability for commodity credits granted by the Bank should be accepted when the claims of other creditors were rejected; if the Bank were unable to write them off, the Bank would have to hold Pakistan liable for them.

The next stage in the negotiations with the creditors was the identification of the 'visibly located projects' in Bangladesh, including the determination of the amount of debt liability based on estimates of total disbursements of credits less repayments up to 31 December 1971. This depended upon the resolution of a number of important issues. First there was the question of defining what was a 'visibly located project' in Bangladesh. The Government defined such a project as one which resulted in the creation of productive assets in Bangladesh and was incorporated in plant, equipment and machinery at the time Bangladesh accepted the liability. This definition excluded imports of spares and components which were not an integral part of the original credit agreement; nor did it include payments for engineering and consultancy services which were not part of the credit agreement establishing the project concerned.

The World Bank sought to take the lead among creditors on these issues and to set onerous criteria for Bangladesh. It advanced a definition which included both spares and components for projects even when these were imported under subsequent agreements, and engineering and consultancy services contracted independently of the original credit agreement. In the event, bilateral creditors were unconvinced by the Bank argument and did not insist on the inclusion of supplies, which were not integral parts of the original credit agreement.

Another issue of importance was the question of damage or destruction of physical assets caused by the war of liberation in 1971. Bangladesh claimed that her total liability should be reduced to allow for such damages or losses. Again the Bank took an extreme creditor position by arguing that the borrower, who was the owner of physical assets, and not the creditors, had to bear the cost of any damage to or loss of assets, irrespective of how such damage or loss was caused. Bangladesh and most bilateral creditors found the Bank's position unacceptable, all the more so as the major losses were inflicted by Pakistan during the war of 1971. In the end all the creditors, including the Bank, accepted that Bangladesh's liability should be reduced to the extent of damages caused by the war.

The problem of how to deal with liability for interest and principal which fell due between December 1971 and June 1974, but which had been rescheduled for payment after June 1974, had also to be resolved. The position of Bangladesh was that this rescheduling was part of the arrangement which the creditors reached with Pakistan in order to avoid Pakistan defaulting. The creditors ultimately recognised this position as valid.

Still another issue related to those cases where credits obtained by the Government of Pakistan, or one of the autonomous agencies of the Government, such as the Industrial or Agricultural Development Banks, were re-lent by them to the Government of East Pakistan or to public sector enterprises or private enterprises or individuals on terms which were harder and for periods which were shorter than the original loan agreements. In these cases, repayments of principal and payments of interest made by the borrowers in Bangladesh exceeded the payments made by Pakistan to the external creditors. Bangladesh claimed that she should be given credit for such excess payments in the determination of her liability. Here again the World Bank initially took an extreme position, but in the end the creditors exempted Bangladesh from such payments.

All parties agreed that Bangladesh would pursue bilateral negotiations with the creditors for the determination of her liability relating to the 'projects visibly located' in Bangladesh. Bangladesh sought to initiate and complete negotiations with the more liberal donors first in order that such agreements could act as a model for the more severe creditors, like the World Bank and Japan. The World Bank, however, was anxious to play the role of co-ordinator and to formulate the negotiating position of creditors as a common approach on issues of controversy. The Bank organised and chaired frequent meetings of the creditors to report progress on the state of negotiations with Bangladesh and for detailed and common examination of the various issues raised in the negotiations. The Bank took the initiative in offering its own advice and guidance to the creditors on a number of these issues. Since Bangladesh found the Bank's position on its loans and credits particularly unreasonable and the Bank's attitudes insensitive and unsympathetic to Bangladesh's own position, this experience of the World Bank as a co-ordinator and leader of aid negotiations was viewed by Bangladesh as an unhappy one.

Behind the blast of argument and counter argument events were slowly being shaped in the second half of 1973 and in 1974 towards the acceptance of a solution to the debt problem. Countries had drawn back from the impasse that had been reached in the March 1973 meeting. The situation cooled, and the initiative taken by Bangladesh in mid-September 1973 to allow negotiation of projects visibly located in Bangladesh greatly helped. Gradually, principles that had been long resisted by creditors found acceptance. Yet, the process of negotiation was protracted. Although donors were most anxious to secure the repayment of the debts they considered owing to them, they were seldom clear what amounts were involved. The flurry and scurry of the March 1973 meeting was succeeded by long periods of waiting for creditors to submit their claims. It was not always easy for Bangladesh to verify these when they did arrive, for much of the documentation needed was not in her possession as it related to loans contracted by Pakistan, and many of the records were not kept in the Eastern part of former Pakistan. At times the records of creditors seemed equally defective. However each claim made by creditors was subjected to careful scrutiny and, gradually, agreed figures began to emerge. By April 1974, the completion of documentation was in sight and there was a prospect that Bangladesh would be in a position to assume liability for agreed amounts by 1 July 1974, the crucial date from the point of view of creditors who had agreed to free Pakistan from obligations to service debt attributable to Bangladesh after that date.

With matters of principle accepted and data agreed, the way was prepared for reaching final agreement. An important aspect of this was the assumption of diplomatic relations between Bangladesh and Pakistan early in 1974; it had always been one of the major difficulties that Pakistan could not hand on the burden of service to a country that she did not recognise. Another issue that had to be resolved before intention could be turned into fact, was the resolution of the terms on which the service obligations would be assumed. Bangladesh had been assured throughout the debt negotiations that the assumption of obligations for existing debt would be followed by debt rescheduling on generous terms. In these respects there were considerable differences of view between the various creditors, which the World Bank helped to resolve; in the end, all bilateral creditor countries were persuaded to offer terms involving a grant element of at least 84 per cent. The final details of the debt settlement were arrived at with the aid of some give and take. The principle of not accepting liability for commodity assistance was adhered to largely on the ground that the local purchasers of such goods, in effect, had made payment already to the Government of Pakistan; no further obligation for payment could arise since purchasers could not in equity be asked to pay twice. At times what had happened and how the principles fitted particular cases was not entirely clear, and so compromises were reached.

It should be noted that the readiness of Bangladesh to accept part of the debt liability incurred by Pakistan was in no way dictated by the urgent need for more aid as the state of economy deteriorated in 1974; the major decision which permitted a solution was the initiative taken by Bangladesh with its aide-memoire in mid-September 1973. The principles on which Bangladesh was prepared to accept a share of the debt incurred by Pakistan followed those already adopted in 1972 for the reactivation of projects and were closely adhered to in all subsequent discussions and negotiations.

The debt issue has faded in importance as time has passed, and as inflation has still further reduced the service obligations accepted; thus it might seem that the preoccupations of an earlier period have little relevance for the future. In the end a solution was found but the underlying issues still remain. Donors sought to impose a burden of debt service on Bangladesh which they had no legal right to do, mainly because they were not prepared to insist on the resolution of their affairs in other ways. Intense leverage was exercised in the process in an effort to force one of the poorest countries in the world to accept obligations that it had not incurred and could not readily afford to take on. The major instrument of leverage was the World Bank and pressure was exerted by threatening to refuse assistance unless the terms that the donors wished to impose were accepted. Sovereign countries are loath to give in to negotiating pressures bordering on threats and Bangladesh, in fact, had little option but to stick to her principles. If ever in the future a similar aid relationship is to move progressively to one of mutual co-operation, attitudes and actions of the type shown by donors in Bangladesh in 1973 must be avoided. With co-operation much can be achieved, but the handling by the World Bank and other creditors of the conflict on the debt issue undoubtedly set back the development of Bangladesh. Moreover, ill-informed and unsympathetic handling of the situation by the Bank strained political relationships and made it difficult to establish those conditions of mutual confidence in which international relations can best work.

Notes

1. A discussion of the quantitative aspects of this issue is to be found in Just Faaland and J. R. Parkinson, *Bangladesh: The Test Case of Development*, C. Hurst & Co., London, 1976, pp. 187–91.
2. It is difficult to infer that the absence of new aid agreements during this period was due to Pakistan's default on debt service payments rather than to the severe disruption of economic activity and great political uncertainty created by the war. Under such extraordinary circumstances, new aid flows for development was unlikely in any case.
3. It so happened that projects financed by the Soviet Union, and the centrally planned economies of Eastern Europe, were almost without exception ongoing projects.

4. This *volte face* was expressed in a letter from the Bank to the Government of Bangladesh at the end of April 1973 which included the following statements:

   'It must clearly be the objective of all those creditor countries to do all that they can to bring about economic and political stability in the subcontinent. Given the circumstances in which these problems have to be considered, it seems clear to me that no action should be taken which would impede a resolution of the problems with which everyone has to be concerned and I have particularly in mind the problems of the relationships between Bangladesh and Pakistan. It seems to me that any diminution of aid to either country at this time might indeed cause difficulties that could make it more difficult rather than easier to achieve these results. . . .

   There is no doubt that the possibility of a default in debt owed to the donor countries presents them with considerable problems, but it seems likely to me that the briefs from which the donor country representatives spoke were drafted with too narrow a perspective and ignoring the longer range economic and political implications. In retrospect, I am sorry that the Dacca meeting came so soon after the Pakistan Consortium meeting in Paris as a result of which it was not possible for me or anyone else to make proper soundings in various capitals. . . .

   However, I hope that all of us will put the events of the past in their proper place so that we can all face up to the difficult challenges that confront us.'

5. Norway and Sweden did not impose conditionality in March 1973: Norway had provided all past aid to Pakistan as grants, and Sweden wrote off its small amount of past loans.
6. For instance, commodities distributed in Bangladesh might have been sent as a *quid pro quo* for commodities sent by Bangladesh to Pakistan or for use of the proceeds of Bangladesh's exports.

10 The Role of the World Bank

JACK PARKINSON

The World Bank is the most powerful international agency concerned with economic development. It is for this reason that some special aspects of the World Bank's influence on events in Bangladesh are examined in a wider setting. Its programmes may or may not be greater than those of other aid-givers but the Bank is invariably regarded by its members as being in the position of giving leadership to their activities. This reflects the prestige that it has built up over the years, based on the high quality of the individuals it employs and its vast and specialised resources. Nowhere else in the world is there such a concentration of talent and know-how directed to the business of development. It has the resources to monitor continually the economies of the countries with which it is concerned and to report on them for the benefit of Bank members; it studies each aspect of the economy in depth and it has the technical knowledge of project preparation and lending for development that can be matched nowhere else.

It might have been thought that Bangladesh would not have hesitated early in 1972 to draw on the Bank's expertise and to have used it as a means to attract assistance from other donors. In fact Bangladesh was in two minds. It regarded the Bank as being subject to strong influence from the United States and, as has been explained in Chapter 2, relations with that country were strained at the time. The Bank for its part was anxious to place its services at the disposal of Bangladesh and prepared to go to some lengths to do so. To have failed in this would have diminished its standing as the leader of the efforts of its member countries' activities in an area of the world presenting a major challenge to development.

It is difficult to trace the early development of relations between the Bank and Bangladesh with completeness. The story at the time, possibly apocryphal, indicated that the first approaches were made in Delhi in February 1972, when Mr. Tajuddin Ahmed, then Finance Minister of Bangladesh, and Mr. McNamara, the President of the World Bank, both happened to be visiting the Indian capital. The Finance Minister was reluctant to meet the President of the World Bank and refused the overtures that were made. The Indian Government was equal to the occasion and skilful enough to arrange that both McNamara and Tajuddin were invited to *Son et Lumière* at the Red Fort on the same day. Strangely enough they were seated together; perhaps more strangely not one word was exchanged. Tajuddin was not amenable to such tactics.

McNamara refused to allow himself to be put off by evidence of reluctance to co-operate and persisted in attempting to establish contact. He succeeded in being invited to Dacca as an official guest of the Government, largely as a result of the personal intervention of the Prime Minister. The ensuing conversation was inconclusive. It was not the Bank that had hesitations but Bangladesh. The Bank is persistent and the approach was pursued, with the result that Bangladesh was eventually drawn into the Bank's orbit. Initially relationships with the Bank, as described in earlier chapters, were strained, but economic necessity and accommodation of attitudes on both sides eventually enabled a smoother working arrangement to be established. When McNamara visited Bangladesh in early 1976, when the Bank felt fully established, he was fêted.

The performance of the Bank is bound to affect the countries to which it lends in a far reaching way and has considerable effect on other donors. A number of aspects of the Bank's activities have been discussed in previous chapters. Here we are concerned particularly with its activities as a co-ordinator illustrated by aspects of its reporting system, its activities in relation to the establishment of a major fertiliser unit within a potential petrochemical complex, and its approach to setting up a population planning programme.

Bangladesh's experience of negotiating with donor countries and agencies acting in concert in 1973 and early 1974 did nothing to belie the doubts that she had felt from the beginning about the wisdom of joining a consortium of aid-giving countries under the chairmanship of the World Bank. The Dacca meeting had demonstrated that donors did indeed seek to co-ordinate their positions and that they did not hesitate to force their views on the countries to which they gave aid. Pressures could be, and were, applied in what appeared to be partial and even arbitrary ways to suit the convenience of major donors. Bangladesh was also acutely aware that its economy was far from functioning normally, and that deficiencies in its administration and management laid the Government open to the exercise of donor influence on the policies which she was pursuing. It was sensitive to the exercise of leadership by the Bank which would be extensive, ranging from matters of high policy to details of the organisation and implementation of projects.

There was often a need to co-ordinate the activities within donors' aid programmes. This could arise when two or more had overlapping interests in developments in particular sectors and might disagree about the approach to be followed, or when in the case of a small sector or project, there was not really room for more than one donor to be involved. Equally there was a definite need for co-ordination when the resources required for a project or a sector of activities were very large and beyond the compass of a single donor. Then the question arose as to how such resources were to be mobilised and how the contributions of the various participants could be integrated. There were many issues to resolve: doubts about the nature of the project itself; differences between donor countries or agencies about who should accept responsibility for the whole or part of a project; uncertainties as to how participants could ensure that their participation met the requirements of their legislatures in relation to accountability; disagreements about the terms and conditions on which assistance would be forthcoming.

For large projects, in particular, there might be differences of view, sometimes amounting to controversy, about the correct approach to follow, with pressures being exerted from both within and without the country, making co-ordination of activities especially difficult. This was evident in the case of the fertiliser and population projects. An important common feature of these projects was that they were too costly to be financed by a single donor so that several had to combine to provide the money needed. Both activities were sponsored by the Bank, although it contributed only a minority share of the finance. The cost and detailed nature of each were worked out over a period of two years and there were numerous discussions with World Bank representatives, as well as with bilateral donors, in which both the Bank and the Government of Bangladesh were involved. The difficulties, as well as the potentials, of co-ordinating project and programme assistance in this way, under the sponsorship of the Bank, were amply illustrated. Different donors have different objectives and different financial procedures. It may be possible for the aid-receiving country to accommodate these within its total aid programme by an appropriate division between donors of activities to be supported; it is much more difficult to accomplish it within the narrow confines of a single project, even one like the fertiliser factory employing standard techniques and with straight forward organisational problems, or a single sector programme, such as the one directed to population planning.

The concern of the Bank with major projects as well as in reviewing the progress of the economy put it in a powerful position. We turn now to its influence on forming opinion in donor countries.

World Bank Reporting

The World Bank has a regular system of reporting on the economies of all the countries to which it gives assistance. At intervals of several years, generally after the preparation of a major medium-term plan, the Bank prepares a thoroughgoing review of a country's affairs. Such basic economic reports are supplemented by others, also covering general economic matters, often prepared at yearly intervals, which form the basis for the Bank's submissions to consortium meetings. In addition, reports are prepared on particular subjects appropriate to the country in question, related in some cases to the identification of areas in which lending might be initiated. No other organisation and no individual donor country prepares reports on the scale of the Bank. They are available to all the Bank's members, are widely distributed and read, and generally are very influential in forming a climate of opinion in donor countries. The Bank has its own ways of organising the preparation of reports which are rather inflexible, as Bangladesh's experience illustrates.

With some exceptions, it is customary for Bank reports to be prepared by teams of specialists from the Bank's headquarters in Washington, who spend a limited period in the field collecting new information and up-dating their knowledge of the country concerned during a visit lasting four to six weeks. This is designed to enable the team to acquaint itself at first hand with the problems of the country and to have the opportunity to exchange views with those concerned with the formulation of policy or its execution. The actual writing of the reports is generally done in Washington, far removed from the country under study. When it was proposed to prepare the first full-scale report on Bangladesh, The Planning Commission expressed to the Bank its preference for an exception being made to the Bank's customary procedures in its case. It was felt that a short visit from outsiders could not give them a full understanding of the problems that had to be faced, however knowledgeable and able such people might be. It indicated its preference for having the report prepared in Dacca by the Bank resident staff reinforced as necessary by additional Bank members or outside experts, as was the procedure adopted for reports on the Indian economy which were prepared in Delhi. Perhaps this represented continued doubts about the ethos of the Bank; it may also have been felt that the local staff residing in the country were likely to have a better appreciation of the social and political conditions ruling. It was understood that the Bank staff in Dacca would be prepared to undertake this task which would have helped to extend the close working relationships based on mutual confidence that had been built up. An arrangement along these lines might well have helped to repair some of the damage to relationships caused by the debt issue and the ill-fated March 1973 Conference.

In the end, the Bank insisted that the Bangladesh report had to be prepared through its customary procedure of having its reports drafted at headquarters in Washington, where the operation could be closely controlled. The dialogue on the Plan which took place between the visiting Bank Mission and the Bangladesh planners and officials during the Mission's visit to Bangladesh was necessarily short. After a few weeks of consultation, the team went back and wrote its report in the Bank headquarters. Subsequently a draft of the report was submitted to the Government for its reaction and comment. The effect the Economic Report produced on the Government has been described in Chapter 8. It may be felt that the incident brings to light a number of important issues on how Bank reports are prepared: the effectiveness of discussions and consultations with the borrowing country during and after the preparation of a report, the extent to which it was necessary for the country and the Bank to agree on its content, the method of presenting such reports, and not insignificantly, the way in which reports of Bank missions are processed and cleared within the hierarchy of the Bank's bureaucratic system before they are made public (albeit for limited circulation of a few hundred copies).

For Bank reports on Bangladesh generally, the experience accumulated that even when powerful arguments were advanced by the Government to show that a commentary in a Bank report was misguided, there was great reluctance on the part of the Bank to acknowledge that the original analysis might have been incorrect. Also on matters of tone and manner of presentation the Bank proved insensitive to criticism and expostulation. As a result, Bangladesh felt increasingly the need for a revision of Bank procedures, which seemed to make no provision for an effective review of such reports by a representative committee of any sort. In the last resort, Vice-Presidents appeared to be formally responsible, but was such responsibility more than a formality? Do they or the area directors responsible for reports really have the time, patience and knowledge to consider reports of several hundred pages in detail and with full understanding of all the issues involved? A great deal, perhaps too much under the present system, is left to mission leaders in matters of substance and form.

The quality of personal relationships are often decisive in interchanges between an international organisation and the countries with which it deals. As judged by the experience from World Bank operations in Bangladesh it appears to be an occupational disease that those institutions and individuals who are responsible for the allocation and administration of aid are liable to regard themselves in some sense as superior to those whose role it is to make use of the resources. The relationship is often an uneasy one – it certainly was so in Bangladesh. The worse the situation of a country may appear to be, the more essential is it to make sure that rapport is established. Those in Bangladesh may be excused for thinking that the Bank should have devoted more attention to the establishment of a basis for mutual respect, and to the development of the Bank's insight and perception of the potentials and constraints of Bangladesh.

In no international organisation, not even in the World Bank, will there be monolithic views on all matters. Different sections, different individuals and different committees may hold a diversity of views. There is, of course, much to be said for giving experts the opportunity to present and argue their own views but when this is done *de facto*, such reports, like academic studies, should be presented in a manner free from any association with any agency or government. Otherwise, they can be exceedingly damaging to the country concerned, with all that implies in its relations not only with the Bank but with other countries which are all too able to 'gang up' in the way described by Mason and Asher.[1] Leverage takes many different forms and the submission of ill-considered and slanted reports is an objectionable instance.

The Fertiliser Project

Originally, what became the fertiliser project had been conceived as a petro-chemical complex, using Bangladesh's very adequate reserves of natural gas. Feasibility reports had been prepared before independence by both foreign and national consultants in the 1960s. In 1970, when the reports were discussed with IDA in the hope that finance could be made available, it was proposed to produce urea fertiliser, synthetic fibre, and PVC (polyvinylchloride). The capacity of the local textile industry was underutilised because not enough imported cotton could be afforded and it was thought that this might be remedied if synthetic fibre could be produced locally.

When negotiations were resumed in 1972, the IDA representatives called for a thorough review of the entire project and the preparation of new feasibility studies. The review recommended that the project should be restricted to the production of fertiliser. It found that only acrylic fibre could be produced, given the composition of the gas; besides involving a dangerous chemical process, this was unsuitable for use in Bangladesh's humid climate. The suggestion was made that an alternative supply of fibre suitable for the textile industry might be obtained by growing cotton or by synthesising polyester from imported oil paid for by the export of natural gas. The production of PVC with the intention of using it is a substitute for corrugated iron or timber for roofing was not recommended.

Based on this review, the World Bank took the position that new feasibility studies were indeed needed, that the production of urea, synthetic fibre and PVC should be considered as separate projects and that it would in any case be impossible to raise enough capital at one time to finance the investment required for all three lines of production; moreover, the Bank concluded, it would be possible to proceed with the construction of a plant for the production of urea well before plans for a more complete project could be finalised. In effect this meant that the World Bank was prepared to sponsor the production of fertiliser but no more. Under pressure the Government accepted the Bank's position, but with the reservation that it would itself seek to raise the finance needed also for the rest of the petro-chemical complex.

The Government explored the possibility of getting help for the construction of the remainder of the chemical complex from the Governments of West Germany, Japan and a number of Eastern European countries.[2] In addition, since the cost of the entire complex was so high as to make it necessary to stimulate interest amongst transnational corporations which, it was hoped, might be able to exert influence on their respective governments to provide credit, the Bangladesh agency in charge of the petrochemical complex, approached private corporations in the UK, US, Canada, West Germany and Japan.

A number of questions raised by the Bank were raised also by the various governments and corporations approached. It was obvious that the Bank had made known its opinions and evaluation on the complex to potential donors and governments and that the Bank's lack of interest in the production of synthetic fibres and PVC clearly affected also their attitudes towards the project.

The capital cost of producing acrylic fibre and PVC on the scale contemplated was found on enquiry to be of the same order of magnitude as that involved in the production of urea alone. Financing on this scale would in fact have required a consortium of the same donors who were expected to finance the urea project. Given this, and the doubts raised by the Bank, it proved impossible for Bangladesh to mobilise the support needed for the whole petro-chemical project. This led to a radical rethinking of the best ways to exploit Bangladesh's natural gas resources, including the possibility of producing additional fertiliser for export within the region, perhaps as a joint project with India, and of exporting natural gas to Japan in liquefied form. Consideration of these matters led to recognition of the need to carry out a full-scale energy survey.

One of the important lessons that was learnt from the experience of trying to get the petro-chemical project financed was that very long delays may occur. Such delays are of considerable importance when costs are rising. While in 1972 the cost of the entire chemical complex was estimated at $350 million with a foreign exchange component of $170 million, two years later the fertiliser project alone was estimated to cost almost two-thirds of the 1972 total and about as much as the original estimate for the total project in 1969. The increases in the cost of the fertiliser project did not alter the view formed at the time the decision was taken to build it, that it would be profitable; the price of fertiliser had risen in the meantime and the estimates prepared showed them to be comparatively insensitive to changes in the assumptions on which they were based.

In the event the project was financed by seven donors who accepted the technical and economic justification prepared by the World Bank without considering it necessary to carry out their own. Japan did not participate in the project, nor more understandably, the centrally planned economies. The main donors were IDA, the Asian Development Bank and the United States, each contributing about $30 million, followed by the United Kingdom with $18 million, West Germany and Iran with $12 million each and Switzerland with $7 million. The credits given by the UK and the USA were tied; other credits were not tied and furnished on IDA terms.

In other respects, the terms on which the credits were made available were more restrictive. Improvements in the production and distribution of fertiliser as a whole had to be made and this involved studying all aspects of the application and marketing of fertiliser, including its price. The Government had to agree in advance to improve the operation of its fertiliser plants and to make every effort to implement the conclusions of the proposed studies as well as to fix the price of fertiliser so that a reasonable return on the equity invested could be obtained.

There are a number of lessons to be learnt from the experience of international co-operation in the construction of the project. The first of these is the difficulty experienced by Bangladesh in being able to approach donors successfully herself. Once the

World Bank took over responsibility for the construction of the plant there was no further room for Bangladesh initiative.

Bangladesh has a number of engineers with experience of fertiliser and chemical plants but would clearly have difficulty in designing and executing a highly technical project on the scale of the petro-chemical complex without foreign technical assistance. An alternative would have been to have asked a foreign country to provide a turnkey fertiliser plan which many might have liked to have done; this was the course preferred by Bangladesh. The Bank, however, was strongly against this solution on the grounds not only that it would be liable to escalate costs, but that it would be difficult to define; they insisted on rigorous standards of performance for the completed project.[3].

The fact of the matter is that a country in Bangladesh's position cannot hope to get money for something as complicated as the construction of a chemical complex, involving the investment of very large sums which have to be raised from a variety of sources, unless she is willing to use the good offices of the World Bank. It is the function of bankers to act as brokers between those who need the money to invest and those who have the capacity to lend it. When providing money they have a responsibility to satisfy themselves of the technical and commercial soundness of the projects for which they raise money and the World Bank is better equipped than most to carry out this function in an international context. This in turn raises another allied question: that of responsibility of bankers not only towards those from whom funds are mobilised, but also towards those who have accepted their technical and financial advice and conditions for going ahead with the project. It is understood that in the execution of the project costs have increased greatly as a result both of inflation and other factors. How an up-to-date cost–benefit appraisal would compare with earlier estimations is not known. If in the process the viability of the project is impaired where in an international world does the responsibility lie?

The Population Project

The need for population planning in Bangladesh is universally recognised, but there was great diversity of view about how best to proceed in this area. There might have been more uniformity of view at the time the Plan was drafted if adequate data had existed for a suitable analysis to be carried out. As it was, no well-considered answers could be given to such questions as whether incentives were necessary to motivate those concerned with advocating family planning, or what forms the incentives, if needed, should take. They might be personal or communal. Would better roads or schools for the community secure a wider acceptance of family planning methods? Should deterrents penalising those with large families be imposed? And so on. The fact of the matter was that nobody concerned with family planning knew much of substance about the form it should take and how it should be organised. This was why the Plan laid great stress on research and evaluation.

Donors had their different opinions on these issues. Some were strongly in favour of using private commercial channels to supplement the distribution of contraceptives, while others would have liked to have channelled a large proportion of their aid to voluntary agencies. These differences of view were second only to those about the appropriate techniques to use for family planning: clinical or non-clinical methods; sterilisation or vasectomy; legalisation or otherwise of abortion and the importance to be attached to it. All this was the subject of hot debate and differing opinions.

The desirability of drawing on international expertise on population matters in an attempt to resolve some of the issues was supported by donors and it was decided that Bangladesh should call an international conference of population planning experts, to evaluate the country's approach to family planning, and suggest how it could be improved. The Conference was held in May 1974 in Bangladesh and aid-givers were prominently represented. It was expected that the views expressed by the participants would carry great weight in the formulation of family planning programmes and crystallise opinion, so that there would be agreement about how Bangladesh should proceed and acceptance of a unified approach by donors interested in supporting activities in this field. It is for this reason that important conclusions reached at the Conference are summarised below, before going on to explain why donors subsequently insisted on following their own individual approaches.

The conclusions reached confirmed Bangladesh's view that allocation of resources for population related activities should depend on the results of the evaluation of programmes and that when these suggested that more resources were needed every effort should be made to make the necessary funds available.[4] The strong case for community involvement was highlighted. It was needed to create a climate of opinion conducive to the establishment of new fertility norms, to involve individuals and local organisations in support of the programme and to bring them into the mainstream of community life; it would provide feedback about how the programmes were going and ensure that the views of villagers and others participating in the programmes would be impressed on those responsible for formulating policies and implementing them. The Conference recognised that such participation and feedback would take time to organise and that in the meantime policies and programmes would have to be devised by the National Government.

It was felt at the Conference that villages would be better served if there were more than one source of contraceptives and numerous volunteers engaged. As a minimum, at least one member of each sex had to be responsible for the distribution of appropriate types of contraceptive. Those most suited for the task were described as being of middle age, themselves users, and preferably of such status that other members of the community would turn to them readily for personal advice. Such individuals might eventually be trained to provide other basic health care services for their villages.

The possibilities of indirect ways of reducing the birthrate were considered at the Conference. If employment opportunities for women could be financed and more support given to general education and the promotion of literacy, it was felt that a favourable climate for population limitation would be created. The idea that family planning could be bought by introducing rewards and penalties was strongly resisted as it had been when the Five Year Plan was prepared. Measures that might be expected at first sight to reduce the birth rate speedily, such as raising the legal age for marriage, were thought likely to succeed only if they gained the force of considerable social acceptance.

The Conference succeeded in clarifying some areas of agreement but differences, some of them important, remained. There was great diversity of views about the best institutional framework for effective action, in particular whether family planning and health services should be integrated in a thoroughgoing fashion under one ministry with complete control of operations, personnel and finance.

Before independence, family planning in Bangladesh had been entirely separate from the provision of health services, using specialised family planning clinics for the promotion of contraception with the aid of semi-literate midwives, and devising its own means of promotion and publicity. In the post-independence period the balance of opinion seemed to shift in favour of the integration of health and family planning services under one ministry. The arguments in favour of this were complex but the most important element in them was that 'face to face motivation' could be done best by those who had been concerned with all aspects of the health and physical welfare of families, through cholera inoculation, smallpox or malaria eradication campaigns or the introduction of better practices of sanitation and hygiene, and who had gained the confidence of the villagers in the process.

In counter-argument, the danger was voiced that when organised within one ministry, health would take precedence over family planning, which would tend to be neglected; there was also the traditional rivalry of the two services to contend with. A powerful argument of the 'anti-integrationists' was that the educational and motivational programme had to be as widespread as possible and to embrace activities by trade unions, cooperatives, farmers associations, adult literacy clubs and campaigns for women's education and welfare – activities which were far beyond the interests of a ministry of health.

The First Five Year Plan of Bangladesh opted for integrated health and family planning services and the use of multipurpose village level workers for the provision of the whole range of health and family planning services. A new Population Planning Division was to be established to co-ordinate the activities of the joint health and family planning service with the relevant educational and motivational programmes of other ministries.

The World Bank was critical of the population programme in general, taking the view that the political leadership was not sufficiently committed to family planning and that too little financial support was to be given to it. Above all, questions were raised about the administrative and organisational framework for the conduct of the programme and its operations. The World Bank argued with some justification, as did others, that it would be unwise to put the Health and Family Planning Division, responsible for family welfare workers and the supplies they needed, under the same Minister as the Population Planning Division concerned with wider issues, since this would tend to reduce the influence and interest of other Ministers who also had responsibility for some aspects of family planning. To counterbalance this, it was argued, it would be necessary for the Planning Commission to continue to vet all family planning projects and decide on the priority to be given to them before expenditure could be authorised.

The need to resolve these issues was reflected in the Credit Agreement made with IDA which laid down exacting conditions specifying the function of the various agencies. The details are not themselves of more than historic importance; the involvement of an aid agency in administrative matters in the borrowing country is the issue of relevance here.

The conditions laid down included stipulations that specific administrative and organisational structures and procedures acceptable to the World Bank had to be adopted. Painstaking negotiations had to be undertaken on the role and functions of the Population Division within the Ministry of Health. The Bank was strongly opposed to the appointment of a medical doctor as head of the Population Planning Division of the Ministry of Health on the grounds that this planning would be dominated by health requirements. At one stage the Bank also tried to impose the general condition that the appointment of the headquarters staff of the Population Planning Division should be subject to the prior approval of the Bank. After negotiation it was agreed that 'The Population Planning Division shall at all times be staffed and managed by persons qualified to insure that the Project will be carried out with diligence and efficiency; and in particular, the head of the Division shall have the qualification and experience required for effective execution of the Project'.[5]

Efforts to intervene in administrative arrangements extended to such matters as the location of administrative units in one ministry or another. Eventually the Bank was persuaded to agree to the location of the Population Planning Division in the Ministry of Health and Population Planning subject to the clause that: 'the Borrower and the Association shall (after one year) carry out a comprehensive review of the administrative and organisational arrangements affecting the project, with a view to determining whether any administrative or organisational changes are desirable in order to accomplish the purposes of the Project.'[6]

As a further condition of the credit, the Government also agreed to conduct a management study of the Ministry of Health and Population Planning with the help of consultants and with terms of reference acceptable to IDA and to implement such recommendations of the study as should be mutually agreed upon; the Government further agreed to carry out a manpower utilisation study in respect of family welfare visitors and female welfare workers, on the understanding that agreed changes in their functions and training would be implemented. In this way, provision was built in for a reconsideration of the design to use multipurpose workers and motivators and for revision of the organisational framework should this be desired.

Another requirement enshrined in the Agreement was a study of the effect on population growth of existing legal provisions and, in particular, the law relating to the minimum age for marriage. Here it is interesting to note that the Bank's appraisal mission for the population project and its general economic mission held quite divergent views: the general economic mission emphasised the importance of immediate legalisation on abortion and other changes in marriage laws, but this view was not shared by the project appraisal mission which was less sure of the answers. Perhaps it is not uncommon for an international organisation to have divided views and to push them both on a recipient country simultaneously.

Some of the matters raised by the World Bank (and also bilateral donors) in respect of the population project were potentially important for the success of the project and it was inevitable that there should be some differences of view which needed to be aired. Nevertheless, attempts to lay down the administrative arrangements that Bangladesh should follow were resented by Bangladesh as amounting to interference in internal arrangements that were not the concern of outside agencies.

The IDA programme included provision of rural health centres, training of nurses and family planning workers, and finance for educational and motivational programmes designed to integrate the operations of five different ministries, in addition to measures to improve the staffing available for family planning in the Planning Commission and research centres and to provide for research and evaluation of the programmes. Other aid-givers interested in population planning were not convinced that the approach proposed by IDA was the best and they insisted on maintaining their individual programmes and approaches. These overlapped to some extent but there was a considerable difference of emphasis between them. The United States, could not be persuaded to support the IDA project which it felt had too many complicating elements and failed to concentrate on its own view that what was needed for population control was to saturate the entire country with contraceptives; and the concern of the IDA project with the construction of rural health centres as a means to spread family planning practices was felt to be mistaken by the Swedish International Development Agency (SIDA).

Irrespective of differences of emphasis in the nature of the programmes to be followed, the large number of donors prepared to support family planning activities raised its own problems. A co-ordinated programme was desirable. An attractive way of doing this might have been for the United Nations Fund for Population Activities (UNFPA) or IDA to have organised a number of integrated programmes co-ordinating all donor activities in this field. Within any family planning programme it was desirable to make use of funds available exclusively for the purpose. The funds of UNFPA for instance, were not available for other purposes and this was also the case for funds provided for family planning activities by US. Ideally, Bangladesh would first use all funds specifically earmarked for family planning and only then consider whether other assistance available for a variety of purposes should also be committed to population projects. In the event, it proved impossible to organize assistance along these lines.

It soon appeared that many donors, including IDA, were not willing to be co-ordinated by the UNFPA. The World Bank, acting through IDA, was willing to co-ordinate the activities of bilateral donor agencies and to negotiate joint or parallel financing of a family planning project with them. For Bangladesh this arrangement offered considerable convenience in simplifying negotiations and avoiding the need for each donor to send an individual mission to appraise the project. It would become the responsibility of the World Bank to convince donors of the value of the project and present it in such a way that it could be easily evaluated by them. However, UNFPA and the World Bank seemed unable to co-ordinate their administration in this way.

Just as the Bank would not have its activities co-ordinated by UNFPA so the latter would not agree that its funds should be used for the IDA programme. Each made their separate and independent evaluations and sent their own appraisal missions to develop projects that they could finance within the general programme.

It took two years to negotiate a project with IDA costing $45 million, reflecting difficulties in formulating worthwhile projects. Although preparation of the IDA and UNFPA programmes started at the same time, agreement with UNFPA was reached nine months ahead of that with the Bank. The reason for this was that UNFPA did not wait to have all the details, including the administrative structure of the programmes worked out in advance of signing. It did not prove possible to integrate the Bank and UNFPA programmes with those of other donors under a unified control.

The UNFPA was strongly against having projects financed jointly by two or more countries or agencies and also disliked parallel financing when different parts of an agreed programme were separately financed. Probably this attitude was a reflection of difficulties it experienced in disbursing funds through the many United Nations' Agencies that executed programmes on its behalf. The project developed by IDA had a major element of joint financing, which was welcomed as conserving IDA money for the finance of commodity imports. IDA provided only $15 million out of the $45 million needed for its programme including money provided by other donors.

In the end Canada, West Germany, Norway, the United Kingdom, Australia and Sweden were persuaded to join Bangladesh in jointly financing the project devised by IDA. The IDA contribution was to be serviced on the usual standard soft terms; the rest of the programme was financed through grants. It proved possible to identify the elements of the programme that the different donors would finance, some concentrating on the construction of buildings and others on the service element. Local and foreign exchange costs were met without distinction. Some of the difficulties felt by Sweden in associating with the IDA project were overcome by arranging parallel financing which permitted Sweden's contribution to particular aspects of the programmes to be identified. Integration was not, however, complete. The Swedes believed that all donors should participate in appraisal and evaluation of projects and this should not be confined to one agency operating on a take it or leave it basis. This attitude led the SIDA to send its own evaluation team before it agreed to participate jointly in the IDA project.

The economic appraisal of the programme was concerned mainly with cost effectiveness and the attainment of organisational efficiency. It was recognised that 'It is difficult with available data at this time to make any meaningful estimates of the project's demographical impact.'[6] It was thought that it might be instrumental in reducing births by 1.3 million during the life of the project and it was speculatively suggested that the total effect by the end of the century might be to reduce births by 23 million with accompanying benefits in child health, which itself would contribute to a reduction in fertility, and other material benefits.

The population project illustrates the difficulties that are experienced in financing projects jointly when it is unclear how best to proceed and there remains a lot of room for diversity of opinion. In an area of activity where most of the problems were at best inadequately understood, the inter-agency bickering among external donors and organisations resembled a situation of the blind leading the blind in comparative ignorance.

Notes

1. Edward S. Mason and Robert E. Asher, *The World Bank since Bretton Woods,* The Brookings Institution, 1973, p. 428.
2. In Rumania fibre was produced from gas (using the cyanide process), but the Bangladesh delegation visiting Rumania found that there was little prospect of Rumania or Eastern European countries financing a petro-chemical complex.
3. The rise in prices evident in 1973 and 1974 would have made it difficult to have arranged a turnkey agreement on the basis of fixed prices.
4. *Recommendations on Population Policy and Programmes*, Unpublished Notes, Seminar on Population Policy of Bangladesh, 15–21 May, 1974, Dacca, Bangladesh.
5. *Development Credit Agreement (Population Project) Between the People's Republic of Bangladesh and International Development Association.* Credit no. 533–BD, 10th March 1975, p. 9.
6. Ibid., p. 14.
7. IBRD/IDA, *Appraisal Report of a Population Project. Bangladesh.* February 1975, pp. 30–31, Report no. 543a–BD.

11 The Role of the Fund

JACK PARKINSON

Bangladesh became a member of the International Monetary Fund in June 1972 and thereby also met a prior condition for membership of the World Bank and its affiliated International Development Association (IDA). In the respective charters of the Fund and the Bank – and even more clearly in the practices that have evolved over the years – there is a division of responsibility and an area of operation between the two institutions. The Bank is concerned with nearly every aspect of the economies on which it reports but it recognises that the Fund has special responsibility for financial matters, both internal and external, and specifically, that the Fund should be accepted internationally as the institution responsible for initiating and conducting discussions about exchange rates.

Over the years, the Fund did in fact provide substantial balance of payments support for Bangladesh; in the process it exerted the full authority of its position in the world on Bangladesh, exploiting its position as a major potential and actual creditor to the utmost. The Fund's exercise in influence on financial and economic policies in the early years of Bangladesh is instructive of the dependence which is inherent in reliance on the Fund and Western sources of finance. In fact, the appropriateness of the exchange rate selected by Bangladesh after separation from Pakistan proved to be a recurrent theme in all discussions held between the Fund and Bangladesh in the early years; but although the theme was unchanging, the economic setting in which it was discussed altered radically as the years progressed.

As a member of the Fund, Bangladesh had access to its resources under normal procedures, as well as to the Fund's special facilities. The quota for Bangladesh in the Fund was fixed at Special Drawing Rights (SDR) 125 million, in 1972 this was equivalent to about US$135 million, which as usual was divided into four equal tranches. Under the standard rules of the Fund, Bangladesh could draw an amount corresponding to the first tranche from the resources of the Fund without difficulty, simply by demonstrating need and active concern to find appropriate solutions to its balance of payments problems, but without the Fund stipulating special conditions. Requests to draw subsequent tranches would involve the acceptance of increasingly onerous conditions as well as higher rates of interest and would normally be available as a stand-by arrangement, the terms for which would be negotiated at the time.

In respect of the Fund's compensatory financing facility, Bangladesh was entitled to assistance if it encountered difficulties as a result of a temporary fall in export receipts. It could be readily established that this was indeed the case; it appeared in 1972 that loans equivalent to two tranches of Bangladesh's quota could be made available. The first of these could be drawn practically unconditionally. It was not entirely clear, however, what would be required in the way of undertakings if Bangladesh decided to draw a second tranche; the requirement formally defined as 'undertaking to co-operate with the Fund' had not been previously interpreted, because no other country had found it necessary to do so at that time; but it was considered that it probably meant nothing more than what was required for first tranche borrowing under the regular operations of the Fund.

Each tranche amounted to SDR 31,250 000 (equivalent to $34 million in 1972), a not inconsiderable sum, and particularly valuable because once drawn it could be fairly freely used. Nevertheless available finance from the Fund was not large in relation to the amount of assistance that was being given from other sources and in other forms; also, the Fund's assistance was subject to politically unacceptable conditions if extended beyond a first drawing. Bangladesh would also be expected to repay her drawings on the Fund within a relatively short period.

From the first, Bangladesh was reluctant to draw on the resources of the Fund because it did not want to place itself in the position of having to accept restrictions on the financial policies it might wish to pursue. In 1972 there was, however, a need to build reserves of international currency, since Pakistan had succeeded in appropriating those that had existed before, export earnings were low, and future levels of aid uncertain. Bangladesh decided, therefore, to explore the possibility of drawing SDR 62.5 million, equivalent to two tranches of its quota, under the provisions of the Fund for the compensatory financing facility. This was really as far as the Government wished to go. Money received in the form of compensatory financing would eventually have to be repaid and if this could not be done out of current earnings it might become necessary to convert the loan by borrowing in the normal way against Bangladesh's quota in the Fund, opening up possibilities for the Fund to exercise financial pressures which Bangladesh might find objectionable. Temporarily, at the end of 1972, reserves were, in fact, unexpectedly high. The Trading Corporation of Bangladesh, the Government's official import agency, had been slow to place orders for imports,, and since deliveries were also slow, the amounts paid out for imports had been much lower than expected. The corollary of the unexpected build-up of reserves was that stocks of imported goods were becoming exhausted and that imports would need to be greatly increased in the future.

A Fund mission visited Bangladesh in March 1973. This was in pursuance of the usual consultations which the Fund had with its borrowing members. It was evident that doubts about the external value of the Bangladesh Taka were expressed. The Fund's reasoning was based in part on a chain of statistical deductions, starting from the presumption that the Pakistan Rupee had been overvalued in 1971, for which there was some evidence in studies that had been made of effective rates of exchange.[1] Bangladesh had not in fact returned to the old parity, equivalent of roughly Tk12 to the pound sterling, but had adopted a new parity of approximately Tk19 to the pound, and therefore could be said to have devalued by one-third. In relation to certain types of export, however, this was more apparent than real: before independence a system of export bonus vouchers had been used to subsidise the export of different commodities by varying amounts, in effect creating a system of multiple exchange rates. Since the export bonus system had been abolished, the effective rate of exchange was in fact little changed on average. A considerable rise in internal prices, relative to those of other countries, had occurred since 1970 and Bangladesh could therefore expect it to be more difficult to find new markets for products previously exported to Pakistan, to develop new types of exports, and generally to expand export earnings. Although the relevance of the statistical reasoning was not immediately apparent, the fact that the Pakistan Rupee had been devalued to approximately Rs26 to the pound sterling was presented as an argument to suggest that Bangladesh should have done likewise.

The position of the Bangladesh authorities at this time was well known: so long as physical and institutional bottle-necks remained the decisive hindrance to efficient and growing export trade, it was neither opportune nor worthwhile to alter the exchange rate. Serious transport difficulties impaired both internal and external trade: roads and bridges, destroyed by the war, were inadequately repaired or replaced; Chittagong port, the most important port of Bangladesh, needed to be completely cleared of sunken vessels; salvage operations in the anchorage in Chalna (the second most important port) had not yet started; inland water transport was also disrupted; the demand for raw jute and jute goods from overseas was strong, but could not be met because it was not possible to arrange timely and regular shipment; in sum, it was not price so much as physical supply on a regular and timely basis that limited exports.

The Government was painfully aware that the jute mills were working at a loss and recognised that devaluation might be expected to improve the position of the industry. But the extent to which this would occur was uncertain; in the circumstances prevailing in 1973, the major result of devaluation might be to create pockets of excess profits in the chain of marketing within the country, rather than to improve the financial position of the mills. The Government judged the effects of premature devaluation on internal prices to be both more predictable and clearly undesirable. After a series of bad harvests the internal price of food had already soared; devaluation could seriously aggravate this unless the implicit subsidy on rationed foodgrains was increased. It would also have effects on the prices of less essential commodities and on the profits reaped from their sale. The rise in prices would have fallen much more on the relatively wealthy consumers of imported goods. In economic equity, this might have seemed to be not a bad thing but in terms of disgruntlement and diminished political support it would have had all the disadvantages of angering a highly influential and articulate minority. The move would also not have been welcomed by business men in the private sector, and it may be judged, by some of their opposite numbers in the public sector who would have found it less easy to sell their wares at the profits of scarcity or with the advantage of conferring favours.

Towards the latter part of 1973, supplies of essential imports were very tight, foreign exchange reserves were low and were expected to fall further; the economy had shown how vulnerable it was to setbacks in agricultural output which increased import requirements. Disbursement of foreign assistance was slow, import prices continued to rise, the money supply had greatly expanded and the general price level had increased by 80 per cent in the period of eighteen months since independence. In the face of such adversity and uncertainty a stand-by arrangement with the Fund was felt to be needed as a cushion against potentially dangerous adverse movements, and Bangladesh initiated discussions with the Fund with a view to drawing the first and possibly also the second tranche of its quota.

Requests to draw on the second tranche of credit have to be accompanied by a presentation of steps to be taken to rectify the situation giving rise to the request. The Government of Bangladesh listed a number of measures directed towards stabilisation of prices and mobilisation of domestic resources. The Central Bank would seek to limit credit expansion during 1973–4 to Tk1350 million and had backed this with the imposition of sectoral limits on major industrial sectors, public enterprises, and the agricultural sector; these limits were to be enforced mainly by moral persuasion on the commercial banks, but advances against stocks of essential goods in scarce supply were prohibited. Import duties on tobacco, cement and iron sheets had been raised, and fees charged on the issue of import licences increased as a step to mopping up scarcity margins. A number of excise duties including those on vehicles, trucks and public carriers had also been raised, as had telephone rates. Subsidies had been reduced by increases in prices of rationed goods: 33 per cent for rice, 89 per cent for sugar, over 50 per cent for edible oil, and 13 per cent for kerosene oil.

It might have seemed that these actions were sufficient evidence of the Government's good intentions to correct financial imbalances. However, it soon became clear that Bangladesh would not be allowed to draw on the second credit tranche without agreement with the Fund on its exchange rate policy. During the discussions with the Fund mission in late 1973, the pressures to devalue intensified. The arguments marshalled at the time for devaluation were the usual ones, echoing those presented earlier in the year. At perhaps a more technical level the additional suggestion was made that devaluation by an adequate margin would provide an opportunity to mobilise resources for development by the simple device of imposing export taxes on jute and jute manufactures, which constituted 90 per cent of exports, rather than by trying to raise revenue exclusively by import duties, always vulnerable to pressure for exemptions and reductions.

The consultations with the Fund's mission in late 1973 also included consideration of the advantages or otherwise of a system of multiple exchange rates. Contrary to the Fund, the Bangladesh Government saw certain advantages in such practices and had already endeavoured to promote new types of exports through an export incentive scheme which permitted automatic permission to replenish imported inputs incorporated in the production of exports of so-called 'non-traditional goods'; exports of jute, whether raw or manufactured, were not assisted in this way. Also a special, more favourable exchange rate for remittances by Bangladesh nationals abroad had been introduced. The Government had in fact a deliberate policy of discrimination between different types of export receipts which, as a matter of philosophy, it seems, is condemned by the Fund as discretionary and inefficient and liable to frustrate the efficient deployment of domestic resources between home and export needs. From the administrative point of view, such a discriminatory foreign exchange policy does have certain disadvantages, experienced also by the Bangladesh Government. Differential measures to increase exports were sometimes rendered ineffective by delays in implementation and suffered from frequent changes unrelated to efficiency criteria. More fundamentally, however, the Fund's objections to reliance on a multiple exchange rate system in Bangladesh were that both traditional and non-traditional exports needed a depreciation of the exchange rate, and miscellaneous potential exports not included in the incentive scheme most of all. The prevailing exchange rate was considered by the Fund to be basically untenable and the differentiation between categories of exports, as applied through multiple exchange rates, without special merit. In Bangladesh's impoverished state few imports were non-essential, it was scarcely possible to think that the application of taxes or special duties on imports would enable sufficient funds to be raised from the market to make good the subsidies needed to ensure the export promotion.

If the argument for devaluation had force, the issue of timing still needed consideration. The Fund considered that the reasonably good harvest at the end of 1973 cleared the way for devaluation early in 1974. The Government, however, continued to fear the inflationary effects of devaluation and did not believe the further incentives were needed to produce more jute or were likely to increase traditional or new types of exports. In many respects neither the Fund nor the Government had changed its position from the previous rounds of discussion in 1972 and early 1973.

Since it could not accept devaluation at that time, the Government requested the Fund to allow it to draw only the first credit tranche of its quota, preferring to do without the second. The Government was prepared to give undertakings to direct its financial policy firmly to reducing the rate of inflation by improvements in budgetary and public sector performance; it was ready to raise interest rates, restrict credit, impose taxes on imports and cut subsidies on food and agricultural inputs, but it was not prepared to devalue as a condition of being allowed to draw the second credit tranche of its quota.

By the summer of 1974 the balance of payments position of Bangladesh had worsened substantially, as described earlier. The request for emergency assistance was immediately referred by donors to the Fund, since it was the agency considered best suited to meeting short-term payments difficulties. Discussions between the Government and the Fund were resumed in July and the issue of devaluation figured prominently. The Fund mission explained that devaluation of an agreed magnitude and with a uniform exchange rate, backed up by appropriate fiscal and credit policies would lay the way open for Bangladesh to have access to two new credit tranches, amounting to $75 million. If, however, the Government insisted on a dual rate system with only a moderately depreciated rate for a limited number of transactions, such as imports of essential items, and a more sharply depreciated rate for the bulk of transactions, this could provide access only to one credit tranche. While the Government and the Fund mission were agreed that devaluation would be inescapable at some point, there were differing views on its magnitude and on the nature and extent of accompanying measures, and most emphatically on its timing.

Over the two years that the exchange rate and export subsidies had been under discussion with the Fund, the magnitude of the changes seeming necessary had increased. This was partly due to a progressive rise in costs and prices within Bangladesh which impaired its competitive position. In mid-1973 the appropriate degree of devaluation had been thought to be about one third, whereas by early 1974 this had increased to over one half. The greater the devaluation necessary, the greater the adjustments to fiscal and monetary policy that would be required.

The Fund strongly advised, as did the World Bank in support, that devaluation should proceed before the consortium meeting in October 1974. This would help, it was alleged, to avoid the impression that the Government was subjected to external pressure, and it would pave the way for the commitment of increased resources from donors. While all these negotiations were being conducted, Bangladesh was progressively entering a famine, for lack of food aid and of foreign exchange resources to buy food in time. This had become all too evident by October. Would Bangladesh be provided with more food aid by food exporting countries if she devalued? It was not clear to Bangladesh whether devaluation before the consortium meeting would result in an increase in overall aid flows or particularly in food assistance; neither the Fund nor the Bank would offer an opinion on this point, except in the most general and vague terms. It was clear, however, that donors were determined to see the devaluation go through and would press strongly for an arrangement to be reached with the Fund.

Bangladesh did not in fact devalue before the October 1974 meeting of the consortium. This made it inevitable that it would form the centre piece of discussions when members met. The terms of the discussion may be imagined easily. Bangladesh might have no control over the effects of import prices, the terms of trade, floods or the breakdown of its biggest fertiliser factory, but it ought to realise that economic policy measures were within the control of government. Exchange rate adjustment was one such policy measure which, if supported by other measures, would right the balance of payments given time. Delay could only exacerbate the situation so that eventual corrective action would have to be more drastic. The system adopted by Bangladesh suffered from all the disadvantages to be expected from multiple exchange rates; the internal value of the currency bore no relationship to its external value, distorting price structures in a way that could not be adequately corrected by price control measures aimed at adjusting comparative incentives to farmers; export prospects would be permanently impaired and development impeded. These and other arguments might readily be culled from economic textbooks.

Pressures generated by words can be answered by words. Discussions at consortia meetings tend to be stereotyped. Bangladesh could reply along well-known and familiar lines, drawing on the standard counter arguments and stressing the physical impediments that were affecting the performance of the economy; it could show the irrelevance of changes in the exchange rate to deal with the life-and-death problem of food shortage and famine.

In many respects such interchanges are mere shadow boxing. Some pledges of assistance were indeed made at the consortium meeting even though devaluation had not been undertaken. Nevertheless there may have been a sense that donors' patience was nearing exhaustion and that Bangladesh might not be treated so leniently at the next meeting of donors if at that time the policies of Bangladesh were still thought to be unsatisfactory, and particularly if the exchange rate had not been adjusted as they required.

While Bangladesh refrained from devaluation, she did in fact receive substantial commitments of assistance, including drawings on a newly created oil facility of the Fund. Further drawings on this facility, however, could not be made without acceding to the Fund's requirements stipulated in the discussions preceding the October 1974 consortium meeting.

The pressure on Bangladesh continued in the month following the consortium meeting. Whenever bilateral aid was being discussed, Bangladesh was made aware that devaluation was expected, and enquiries were made as to whether she had reached an understanding with the Fund. In March 1975 there was a visit of a Fund mission to Bangladesh and during the ensuing discussion the government agreed to devalue the exchange rate by 58 per cent. As part of the arrangement Bangladesh obtained an assurance by the Bank and the Fund that they were ready to do their utmost to mobilise greater resources. The Fund would make available under its own arrangements a credit of $75 million corresponding to two credit tranches (the second and the third, the first having been drawn earlier) as well as access to the oil facility for an amount of nearly $20 million.

The economic and financial position of Bangladesh was reviewed in discussions with the mission to determine what package of measures was appropriate to the new situation. Financial measures stipulated by the Fund included strict scrutiny of requests for additional credit by public enterprises as well as increases in interest rates, and limits to credit expansion at four specific dates during 1975–6. Both parties recognised that the most important inflationary factor at the time was inadequate food production and that financial policies can do little to prevent prices from increasing when there is a harvest failure. The declared objective of the Government of reducing the rate of general price increase from as much as 75 per cent in 1974–5 to 10 per cent in 1975–6 was based on the assumption that food production would increase satisfactorily.[2] This declaration was to be backed by a set of measures to control inflation; in particular restraint was to be exercised on wages and salaries, although some adjustments would be necessary to cushion the effects of devaluation on the rise in the cost of living. While the Government encouraged State enterprises to pass on to consumers any increase in costs due to higher import prices, there remained the vexed issue of the subsidy on foodgrains which, it was agreed, should be reduced gradually. Subsidies on agricultural inputs would be terminated, except when necessary to ensure the use of new technologies.

Government finance was a key area for discussion. Here decisions were taken to impose export taxes on raw jute and jute manufactures, which could be flexibly administered and provide a means of distinguishing between traditional and non-traditional exports; in a small way it amounted to introducing a system of multiple exchange rates. The yield of taxation was to be maintained by introducing *ad valorem* rather than specific duties, as well as by widening the net of direct taxation. Bangladesh was required to give an assurance that, even in emergency situations, it would avoid incurring debts of less than five years maturity to purchase foodgrains and other essentials, and to limit other debts of less than fifteeen years maturity.

Inefficiencies in the administration of the import system were acknowledged and some agreement reached on steps to be taken to effect improvements, including the earlier announcement of import licences for the coming period, longer validation of licences and, as soon as the foreign exchange position would warrant it, extension of the licensing period from six months to a year. Also licences were to be issued in amounts which took account of price changes and on the basis of actual utilisation of capacity rather that on a one-shift basis, as well as in broad commodity groups rather than for specific items which was deemed to have been too inflexible a system. In the Fund's pursuit of a more market oriented system, efforts were to be made to place most essential items on open general licence, as soon as the foreign exchange position eased. The Government was pressed to agree to seek to revert to direct importation where feasible, rather than to rely on the Trading Corporation of Bangladesh which was not well regarded by Western donors.

Bangladesh undertook to devalue, having reluctantly come to the conclusion that if she did not, total assistance would be less than it was. There is no way of proving that this would have been the case, given the way the aid was pledged; what is significant is that the total amount of aid ultimately committed was considerable. Equally important was the greater readiness of donors to provide commodity assistance, which together with food aid, came to 75 per cent of the total; commitment of food remained high at 1.5 million tons, less than the amount asked for but a generous response nevertheless.

Was the timing of devaluation correct? Opinions differed on this. If Bangladesh had devalued in August 1974, she would have obtained immediate access to about $75 million from the IMF. In view of the grave crisis of food and finance at the time, this could have helped significantly. It was more doubtful whether bilateral donors would, or could, have provided more than they actually did in late 1974. On the most important question of food supplies in late 1974, decisions by major food exporting countries could hardly have been affected by the delay in carrying out devaluation. However a devaluation in 1974 would have effected a desirable change in the relative price of jute in time for the cultivation of jute for 1975 season: sowing was in early 1975 and the relative price in late 1974 was a determining factor in the amount of acreage devoted to jute.

In retrospect, what was remarkable in the debate on the value and importance of devaluation and its timing, was the force of conviction of outsiders that devaluation was the single most important reform to be made in economic policy. To many policy makers in Bangladesh the emphasis by the Fund and donors generally on devaluation as the 'acid test' of economic management and development was a considerable exaggeration. From the perspective of Bangladesh, mobilisation of domestic resources, including the elimination of subsidies, reduction in deficit financing and generation of a surplus by the public enterprises, were as important if not more so; by far the greatest need was improvement in social organisation and economic management, particularly in the fields of agriculture and nationalised industries. Devaluation can be accomplished by a stroke of the pen, but other improvements and reforms take time to carry out. Devaluation of the Taka was a necessary but not a sufficient condition for an improvement in the balance of payments. The measures on the domestic front needed greater commitment and more dispersed action and would take time to produce their effects. A dialogue on these measures should have preceded devaluation; the timing of the devaluation itself – as well as the timing of any pressure by the Fund and the donors for devaluation – should have been determined in the light of progress made in achieving a consensus on the range of measures that are needed to make devaluation effective.

Notes

1. See, for example, Mati Lal Pal, The Determinants of the Domestic Prices of Imports, *The Pakistan Development Review*, Winter 1964, p. 597; Mohiuddin Alamgir, The Domestic Prices of Imported Commodities in Pakistan: A further study, *The Pakistan Development Review*, Spring 1968, p. 35 and Stephen R. Lewis Jr., *Economic Policy and Industrial Growth in Pakistan*, George, Allen and Unwin, London, 1969, pp. 154 and 159.
2. It did, and this explains why in spite of devaluation food prices declined in 1975–6, the first year after devaluation.

Part Four:

Aid and Dependence

12 The Lessons

JUST FAALAND

It remains to review and interpret the lessons to be learnt from the experience of relationships between Bangladesh and the international aid community in the period 1972–5. Bangladesh was put in the position of having to create a national state at a time of great economic difficulty. The problems were extremely severe and could not be speedily resolved, it has taken time and a series of consecutive good harvest conditions to get the economy onto an even keel, and it has required large amounts of international assistance for it to be accomplished. For the international community and for the United Nations system it has been a period of trying to establish sound and effective aid relationships. Bangladesh's hesitations about the extent to which she was prepared to rely on assistance from the West, understandable as they were, made her question whether traditional donor – recipient relationships were the best that could be devised and whether they were well adapted to dealing with the needs of poverty stricken applicants for aid. At the same time, some bilateral and multilateral donors with strong, and at times inflexible, views about what they expected of Bangladesh, seem to have been unaware of the damage that they were doing, not only to that country but to themselves as well, by the force and form of pressures that they were exerting. The period was as much a test of their performance as it was of that of Bangladesh.

The opportunity for the aid-givers to impose their views on Bangladesh was made all too clear when it became the accepted view that Bangladesh simply could not manage her economy without the assurance that large amounts of aid would be forthcoming. The influence of donors is inevitably much greater, and the leverage that can be exerted correspondingly more intense, when a country is considered to be unable to function without aid. When this happens special measures may be needed to protect it from donor interference: when the economy was on the verge of collapse the resistance of Bangladesh to many donor impositions ceased.

It is true that this has made for an easier working relationship, but patterns once set are not readily reversed. For Bangladesh, reliance on outside assistance is most likely to be a feature of the development of the economy over many years, if its problems are to be solved. All countries experience some loss of independence if they cannot avoid heavy dependence on aid. The full extent of this is difficult to appreciate without a detailed understanding of what is involved in individual cases and of how officials and aid agencies influence events. This is one reason why studies of the World Bank's operations, in particular those of Mason and Asher and of Escott Reid,[1] are an indispensable element in appreciating the issues involved. These need to be matched by studies of the experience of individual countries receiving aid to reveal the interplay between aid-givers and receivers and to widen the perspective as this book seeks to do.

All these relationships have a common thread. Many less-developed countries find it difficult to establish stable systems of government and to build up managerial capacity. Until they can do so they are vulnerable to pressure and in ways that it is not always easy for individual countries or agencies to appreciate. Sometimes pressures are the cumulative results of individual requirements insisted upon by donors without realising that, if all do so, the country concerned will be adversely affected in the process. All countries and agencies are naturally keen to ensure the success of their own activities and to enhance the specific contribution that they expect to make to the development of a recipient country, and they have a duty to those for whom they act to ensure that the funds they dispense are well used. Often this means that they wish special consideration to be given to the activities that they are supporting, for instance by trying to insist that the projects with which they are concerned are directed by the best administrators, that they have a ready supply of the inputs they need, and generally that they are operated in an efficient way so as to ensure success. When all agencies seek to do this, the resources of the country in the form of able administrators and scarce inputs may not be enough to go round; moreover, those formulating policy may find so much of their time taken up with meeting the needs of donors that the functioning of other, sometimes more important parts of the economy, may be impaired. It may also leave the way clear for the suppliers of goods furnished under aid to exercise their influence unchecked by the normal constraints of administrative processes.

In other ways also, those who administer the provision of aid may not have as full an understanding of the functioning of the country and its economy as is needed. Sometimes they realise this, often they do not appear to do so. Economists brought up in the Western tradition do not hesitate to advocate general and specific policies to improve the functioning of the economy of the recipient country. In Bangladesh, as elsewhere, many do so with a show of conviction and assurance, far too often exhibiting arrogance combined with authority derived from their being representatives of agencies and interests with large resources. It was not difficult in Bangladesh to argue the general case that the economy would work better if the Taka were devalued, or if more resources were raised in taxation, or if administrative skills were improved, or rewards and retribution were brought to bear. However unjustified, it often seemed to be assumed by economists, bankers and other experts from abroad that those responsible for directing the economy were unaware of what was needed, or that they might not wish to take remedial action at the appropriate time and in a way best adapted to the needs of the country. The pressures of repeated criticisms, as echoed from many mouths, can prove counterproductive and may actually build up resistance to change rather than promote it.

Mistakes, of course, were made. But it was not only those in Bangladesh who made mistakes in the policies that they followed. The international community was slow to appreciate that initially the provision of project aid, and even the reactivation of projects already started, would add little to the desired flow of resources into the country and contribute little to the development of Bangladesh in the short-run, or indeed in the longer-run, if this meant that the resources for the efficient operation of the economy were not forthcoming on the scale required. Even to-day, donors are likely to cling to the view that it is projects that create investment, and investment that creates income. Some friendly critics argued, and justifiably so, that Bangladesh's own planners erred in this direction in proposing in the First Five Year Plan a development effort that the country could not be expected immediately to sustain. In fact very little of the progress registered by the economy even in recent years is due to project implementation in the sense of setting in train new developments. Large amounts of project aid have been made available to Bangladesh, but disturbingly little of it has been disbursed. Progress, such as it is, has come from making better use of existing resources and by improving economic organisation, and it has been decisively sustained since 1975 by favourable weather conditions that have allowed agricultural output to rise to record levels.

The issue of judging what is needed for an economy goes much deeper than the making of economic programmes. It is not easy for any person foreign to the country in question to develop the understanding and knowledge of the people, customs and aspirations to be able to identify the best policies to follow and those that stand some chance of acceptance. Few advisers are equipped with the empathy, patience and modesty to put over their point of view even when it is soundly based. Strains are particularly liable to arise when highly qualified representatives of aid-giving agencies impress on their opposite numbers in the recipient country the desirability of carrying out the policies that their organisation stands for at the time. Discussions between technocrats are always liable to be heated and may be conducted as though they were academic interchanges. It may well be argued that the art of the development diplomat is much more difficult to master than other types of diplomacy and can all too easily be forgotten when officers of different experience are called upon to talk, or negotiate, on an equal footing. Such officers 'are not protected, as are national diplomats, by the consciousness of belonging to a profession which has worked out codes of conduct to ease the strains of inter-state relations.'[2]

The final straw in all such interchanges is when donors become so convinced of the rightness of their positions that they cannot brook failure to get their way, and if all else fails, resort to threatening to cut off the supply of assistance. These aspects of the difficulties encountered in aid relationships can be abundantly illustrated from the experience of Bangladesh, as has been done in the previous pages. They are not confined in any way to that country. The arrogance of technocrats travels round the world.

The attempts of bilateral donors to persuade recipient countries to see things their way can be greatly reinforced if coordinated into collective leverage. The World Bank would not be the power it is if it had no more influence than the dollars it can bring to bear. It seeks to enhance its influence by organising and co-ordinating the activities of other donors and convincing them of the rightness of recommendations. Busy officials in many countries rely on the analyses and opinions of the Bank and it is liable to be regarded as a depositary of sound ideas and judgment. There are dangers in relying on paradigms; development is not an exact science and diversity of views is desirable if development is not to be swayed by temporary changes in fashions. Ideas concerned with the desirability of concentrating on industry or agriculture, on import replacement or export promotion, on the public or private sectors, on infrastructure or basic needs, come and go with the appointment of the World Bank presidents and senior officials (with few exceptions from Western countries only), and establishment economists and special advisors from governments and universities. There is truly the need for wise men, independent of institutional pressures or the need to make their own names and under no compulsion but to achieve the common good, to reflect at ease on the development requirements of individual recipient countries. In this process there might also be much to be said for seeking wisdom from those in developing countries as much as from those of the West. It is interesting and disturbing that the accepted development philosophies and fashions being followed by aid-givers, and the policies for structural as well as short-run change urged on the less-developed countries by such international agencies as the World Bank and the IMF, owe very little to experience and thinking emerging from the developing countries themselves. The objectives and the strategy of directing development efforts so as to meet supposed basic needs of the community are much more associated with the international agency establishment and its leaders, spokesmen and apologists, than with the policies advocated by developing countries.

Donors are always in a position to consult one another, whether formally or informally, and they organise their affairs collectively in a variety of ways. The influence of Western donors is uppermost in the councils of the World Bank and of the Fund; they also meet in the Development Assistance Committee (DAC) of The Organisation for Economic Cooperation and Development (OECD) in Paris. In the case of a large number of aid-dependent countries, the Western donors meet and co-ordinate their views in so-called consortia or aid groups; when such institutions do not exist, donors co-ordinate their aid relationships in informal meetings organised by the World Bank and through ordinary diplomatic interchanges. Donors can readily co-ordinate their views and organise a collective stance if important members in their midst feel this to be necessary. The opportunities for them to exercise leverage are correspondingly great. Their influence is likely to be all the more powerful and domineering if they believe that they are acting in accordance with a sense of collective wisdom, to which all right-thinking persons should subscribe.

The facilities available to the less developed countries to meet and review their interests are not developed on the same scale, or with sufficient cohesion, or in a sufficiently concentrated fashion for them to be as effective as those of the developed countries. There is nothing, for instance, that mirrors the collective activities of donor countries meeting as a consortium to review the performance of a single recipient country. Yet if it is right for donor countries to assume a collective obligation for helping those in need, should there not also be meetings resembling those held by consortia to review the progress of individual donors in meeting the requirements of the less developed countries? Might it not be appropriate for, say, the countries of South Asia to arrange their own meetings at which each of the DAC member countries could be asked to explain the reasons why their aid programmes to the region should not be increased, why the terms of aid should not be improved or why onerous conditions should be imposed? It is all too easy to assume that obligations lie with those that receive and never with those that give.

If collective leverage by donors is to be exerted there must be acceptance by them of group leadership and active adherence to a prevailing view. The ways in which this can be brought about have been illustrated by the experience of Bangladesh. The power of the Fund in insisting on devaluation is very great once countries need to borrow from it. Donor countries and agencies have accepted that it is the prerogative of the Fund to pronounce on these matters and that its view should be accepted by donors and recipients alike.[3] Individual countries are seldom likely to interest themselves in such issues or at least to analyse them in depth; in fact, they readily adhere to what the Fund recommends.

It is of importance for an understanding of these relationships to register that when the Fund in its own wisdom had decided that Bangladesh had to devalue and when the Fund also found itself in a position to enforce its wishes, the insistence on devaluation was strongly echoed by all Western countries who considered themselves concerned with Bangladesh's affairs.

Much the same convergence of attitude was evident in the case of the Pakistan debt issue, though not all countries were directly affected by it. Most of the countries were owed money by Pakistan, but had it not been for the World Bank it is very unlikely indeed that they would have raised the issue in the manner and with the vigour that they did, and with so little understanding of the political ramifications of the issue and of the reactions that it aroused. The Bank has been dominated from its inception by the fear that the loans it made might not be repaid with interest. This is as understandable as it was inevitable, since the Bank for its traditional lending operations depends on raising capital on the open market and must therefore be concerned to maintain confidence in its ability to invest in financially sound projects and thus to meet its own obligations. Interest and repayment on its loans must be paid by its clients in time and in full, although in many instances re-scheduling of other debts had to be resorted to in order to prevent default. To the establishment of the World Bank it undoubtedly seemed unreasonable that Bangladesh was not prepared to accommodate it and agree without more ado to accept what the Bank itself judged should be Bangladesh's share of Pakistan's debt liability to the Bank and indeed to other creditors as well. The Bank clearly considered that its indication that debt assumed by Bangladesh would be rescheduled on generous terms, and with the promise of more aid to follow, should have been sufficient to persuade Bangladesh of the wisdom of submitting to the Bank's judgment. In the event, the Bank and the other creditors who followed its leadership greatly misjudged the position. Bangladesh was not in a position in 1972/73 to make what would have amounted to a major political concession to Pakistan, when so many issues remained to be resolved by political means. When the creditors in 1972 and 1973 made their ill-considered attempts to secure acceptance by Bangladesh of part of Pakistan's debt, before recognition had been conceded by Pakistan, it was evident that Bangladesh would have preferred to be struck off the list of recipients of development assistance from foreign donors rather than to make the political concessions that acceptance would have required.

This incident raises a number of general issues. The first is whether there is justification today for the Bank's assumption that it should be regarded as a preferred creditor in order to maintain its status on the world's money market. To governments this may seem to have some advantages, because part of the funds required to assist the developing countries with development may be raised from the private sectors of the member countries of the Bank, thus relieving their treasuries of the necessity of greater government borrowing and allowing additional funds to be raised from those capital markets with resources available. The loans raised by the Bank are made under the guarantee of the member governments of the Bank, so it is to them that creditors may look in the last resort. Even so the Bank may feel more secure if the question of its having to make use of such guarantees is never even remotely in question. Perhaps as some halfway house, arrangements could be made in case of difficulty for the service of Bank debt to be undertaken out of a special fund subscribed by Bank members. The issue of debt service is likely to come up in relation to a number of countries for which service payments have been mounting and may require some unified approach.

Devaluation and the debt issue were two instances where there was unanimity of view, or at least acquiescence, among Western donors. In the case of the population project, important though it was as an attempt to tackle the problem at the root of Bangladesh's difficulties, there was no monolithic view among donors on how it should be pursued. There was no question in these circumstances of other than bilateral pressure being exerted on Bangladesh. For Bangladesh, if she had been so inclined, it could have been a clear case of divide and rule. In contrast, Western donors did not question the judgment of the World Bank in respect of Bangladesh's proposals for a petro-chemical complex. Potential sources of finance fully accepted the technical and financial leadership of the World Bank in this project; and they did not hesitate to limit their assistance to only that part of the complex which was favoured by the Bank.

There is little that countries receiving aid can do to contend with the dominance of co-ordinated donor positions in such matters. Dependence on aid from major Western countries and their institutions impose limits on the flexibility of choice between options and on the autonomy of the government and institutions in developing countries. But what is the justification for involvement of donors in this form and to this extent in the affairs of aid-receiving countries? Do they not know their affairs best; cannot they be trusted to use resources placed at their disposal to the best advantage? No categorical answer can be given to either of these questions. It is normal to find very differing views in any country about the appropriate policies to follow. The policies being pursued at any given time by a developing country may be subject to modification and if in the eyes of donors there are better alternatives available they may be tempted to hasten the process of change. Sometimes this may be beneficial but it cannot be assumed that it will invariably be so and the chances of a successful outcome are generally not high enough to justify attempts to intervene in a grand manner.

On some major issues the points of view of aid-givers and receivers may be far removed. For Marxists, development means 'transforming the Third World along communist or socialist lines. For the West, it meant developing poor countries along liberal, democratic lines. For the Third World, it meant obtaining external assistance in choosing developmental models best suited to their peculiar circumstances.'[4] Aid is bound to be regarded as an important instrument in such ideological confrontations. 'Security assistance' is always likely to take priority over development consideration in the US food credit programme under PL 480, and Kissinger explicitly made this clear to government policy-makers in 1974.[5] Some would maintain that rich countries, contrary to what is so commonly supposed, do not have any moral or religious obligation to come to the aid of poor countries; there are no parallels, the argument goes, between the gifts of individuals as charitable acts and the actions and obligations of governments and states.

It is hard to argue that donor countries 'know best' in relation to political issues and it is even more difficult to argue that they are in a position to judge issues in which economic considerations are deeply entangled with social forces and political motivations. Donors to Bangladesh were all too ready to get involved in such complex relationships. In certain technical respects donors do know best because they command expertise and technical know-how beyond the immediate reach of a developing country. The issue here is who should be put in the position of calling on the expertise, the donor or the recipient. Bangladesh felt very strongly that it should be for her to draw on technical assistance rather than for those financing a project to furnish it for her. A distinction should also be drawn between the making of policy governing economic development, which is essentially the province of the developing country itself, and actions taken within the context of that policy: the strategy for industrial development is a matter for the government of the country concerned; the execution of that policy, in the sense of providing equipment and expertise, however, may well be something it wishes to arrange via foreign suppliers and technicians.

If anything, there seems to have been a tendency over the years for the donors to exercise increasing involvement in decision taking, aid used to be regarded as essentially a catalytic means to advance development. Now aid-donors seem to require detailed discussions and participation in every aspect of the activities they help to finance. There would be something to be said for trying to put this into reverse and to reduce donor involvement to the minimum. The obstacle to doing this is that donors have responsibility as well as objectives. They have an obligation to seek to ensure that aid is not wasted, but is used efficiently and as required by their legislation. Thus in bilateral aid relationships detailed agreements as to the ways in which aid is to be used (with supporting conditions or side letters) may be an unavoidable condition of giving aid in the first place. The alternative of channelling assistance through multilateral agencies may be even more exacting in some respects, as Bangladesh's experience has shown; it sometimes tends to be combined with an exercise of expertise more of instruction than of helpful counsel. At times it may almost seem, when a visiting mission descends on a country, that the foreman of works has come to inspect the progress made since his last visit. This may be more a matter of style, and therefore correctable, than of substance, but it has given rise to a number of proposals for changed working relationships.

In the first few years of its existence Bangladesh undoubtedly benefited from donor co-ordination through the United Nations. The response of the United Nations to its needs not only in providing resources but also in organising the distribution of them within Bangladesh was of great importance and value in a situation where the administration of the country was disrupted. The establishment in more recent years of specific machinery to co-ordinate the activities of donors in Bangladesh has had much less marked advantages.

It is arguable that the issue of a consortium for Bangladesh should be seen less as an attempt to exercise collective leverage than as something that suited the convenience of the World Bank more for its own prestige, status and perceived importance and effectiveness. While it is true that consortium meetings give donors opportunities to expound and impose a collective view on the recipient country, it is also true that such a view often emerges from the reports prepared for them by the Bank, from which most of the participants are likely to take their cue. This is not peculiar to consortium meetings; donors incline to the Bank line whether a consortium has been established or not.

By their nature consortia are donors' institutions; only imperfectly and sporadically can they be expected to promote the interests of those receiving aid. Most donor countries and agencies do not, for example, use the occasion of a consortium meeting to give assurances of aid for more than the most immediate future, whereas to the aid-recipient commitments for a period of years would be of great help in the planning process. In this respect it is not so much the reluctance of consortia to do so, as the fact that national legislatures are often not in a position to commit funds for more than a year at a time.

There is no evidence in the case of Bangladesh that the establishment of a consortium increased the flow of aid, although it is possible that it may have encouraged Japan to assist Bangladesh more generously. It is true that commitments of aid have been at a high level in recent years but in real terms they have not been much, if at all, greater than they were in the first few years of the resumption of aid programmes. Such comparisons cannot be of more than limited relevance. It is possible that the certainty with which aid can be assumed to be forthcoming is increased by regular meetings of donors, and that in consequence the economy can be planned with greater assurance, but even this seems doubtful. The existence of a consortium at the time of the Cuban incident in the spring and summer of 1974 would very likely have done nothing to ensure replacement supplies of food from non-US sources or to protect against other forms of political action by major donors.

Much the same applies to issues relating to the conditions on which aid is made available. Bangladesh was not assisted in this way by the consortium. Liberalisation of the terms on which aid is made available owes much more to discussions between members of DAC of the OECD on general relationships between rich and poor nations and on the strategies and the principles of the application of aid in its various forms to different categories of recipients, than it does to the conclusions of consortia-type meetings. Similarly, the decision of the World Bank to allocate IDA funds to the poorest countries, including Bangladesh, was not the result of consortia meetings or of specific efforts to soften the terms of lending to Bangladesh. In other ways consortia meetings are singularly void of value to countries in need of aid. They have done nothing to simplify and standardise procedures for the disbursement of aid, which for Bangladesh would have been of considerable value, and they have done very little to resolve issues related to tied aid generally and to the particular needs of recipient countries when the interests of aid recipients have been at variance with those of donors. In short, it is a conspicuous feature and major defect of the consortium approach that it is lopsided, mainly directed to examining the case of the aid-recipient while doing little systematically to put pressures on aid-providers to increase the volume and efficiency of their aid, for example by modifications in their aid procedures.

A number of suggestions, old and new, were put forward in the case of Bangladesh to make the operation of a consortium more acceptable to it. It was suggested, for example, that it would be better if it were not chaired by the World Bank: a notable exception to this had been made in the case of Indonesia where the Dutch provided the chairman. More generally, it might be preferable to appoint some independent person of prestige to chair consortium meetings. In addition to chairing the meetings he might travel to the capitals of donors to seek to persuade their governments to increase the volume and improve the quality of their assistance to and cooperation with developing countries generally, and with specific consortium countries in particular.

The glaring fact has been brought out repeatedly that the directing influences of the World Bank are not fully representative of the countries, recipients as well as donors, concerned with economic development. Escott Reid has pointed out that in 1973 of the 80 senior officers listed in the organisation chart published in *Bank Notes*, 45 per cent were United States citizens;

five years later little if any change in this type of bias has been brought about.[6] As some counterweight to this accumulation of influence the suggestion has been made that it would be advantageous for Executive Directors to serve for longer terms in order to make their advice more effective. As presently constituted, however, an executive director representing a borrowing country is unlikely to be overcritical of the Bank's policies and operations because it might be feared that this would adversely affect the borrowing opportunities for the country he represents.

Another approach to decreasing the influence of entrenched management attitudes might be to limit the term of office of those holding senior appointments to, say, no more than five years, thus arranging a rotation of staff of different views, persuasions and personal aptitudes. This might give an opportunity to employ a greater proportion of staff from aid-receiving agencies with the actual experience of guiding economic development. In this respect also it might reduce the tendency on the part of those responsible for aid administration in those countries, to operate in relation to aid agencies in the knowledge that they might wish to make their ultimate career in the World Bank. They would be able to work with the Bank, but only for a limited period. The argument also applies to other international organisations operating in their respective special fields. A further advantage of this arrangement might be that the best minds in the developing countries would not be permanently lost to the countries from which they originate, which happens all too often with the present system.

Other suggestions for improvement have also been made, including a stronger and more numerous representation of the country presenting its case at the consortium meeting relative to the representation of donors. Such suggestions have sometimes been coupled with pleas for greater reliance by donor countries and international agencies on administering aid regionally or in recipient countries, in an effort to avoid so much influence on recipient countries from the capitals of major donors, in particular from Washington, the headquarters of the World Bank and the Fund, which are so clearly and so often exposed to the influence of the US Government and American interests.

Recently some proposals for reform have been made which take on a more fundamental character. There have been suggestions that a new international organisation should be established with its own sources of revenue and independent direction to development. Finance for such a venture might be provided by the operation of the 'link' so that special drawing rights would be placed at its disposal, or by taxes on natural resources, particularly those not already in national possession, notably those available from the ocean if techniques and necessity direct mining to that area. Less realistically, perhaps, taxes on armament expenditure have been proposed. Still another suggestion is the desirability of imposing an international tax on rich individuals following perhaps a Muslim philosophy that the rich as a matter of obligation should pay $2\frac{1}{2}$ per cent of their assets to the poor (Zakat). Since action along these lines may not find acceptance, more practicable ways to reform may require administrative changes in the direction and functioning of existing institutions by elaborating some of the proposals discussed above.

The general issues that have been raised in our account of the Bangladesh experience in aid and influence need also to be seen in relation to the demands for the establishment of a new international economic order, NIEO. As we have seen, the provision of aid is at present subject to the tight control of donors. There is overwhelming evidence of very considerable intervention in the domestic and external affairs of aid-recipients, which can hardly be thrown off once a country has accepted a strategy for development based on a continuing flow of resources from abroad; it becomes well nigh impossible to draw back. Bangladesh, like other recipient countries, would benefit from adoption within NIEO of some of the specific proposals being discussed, but on balance Bangladesh would be unlikely to be very favourably affected: what might be gained in relation to commodity stabilisation for jute might well be lost by arrangements to sustain levels of the price of food and raw materials. Demands for further trade liberalisation could conceivably have considerable effect on Bangladesh's export earnings in the future, but it would be of little relevance to its needs today: it will take time to build the country's capacity to exploit such market opportunities in advanced countries.

For Bangladesh, as for some of the other developing countries there is really not very much alternative to aid dependency, or relief in prospect from exposure to the influence of donor countries and agencies. This makes it all the more important to increase the flow of resources from rich to poor countries and to learn to accept the lessons of experience of the nature and extent of influence by aid-providers on decision making, which sovereign nations rightly consider their own prerogative.

Notes

1. Edward S. Mason and Robert E. Asher, *The World Bank since Bretton Woods*, The Brookings Institute, 1973. Escott Reid, *Strengthening the World Bank*, The Adlai Stevenson Institute, USA, 1973.
2. Escott Reid, op. cit., p. 93.
3. This might not be so if the other Bretton Woods organisation, the World Bank, were to take a different view from that of the Fund, but in practice the two agencies have divided responsibility and work between them quite clearly, and each appears fully to support the positions of the other.
4. Gerald Caiden, *Administrative Reform: A Prospectus*. Paper presented to the Third Annual Hendricks Symposium, University of Nebraska, Lincoln, 1978.
5. See the *Washington Post*, 30 September 1974.
6. Escott Reid, op. cit., p. 190.

Index